Getting Work with the Federal Government

A guide to figuring out the procurement puzzle

MARION SOUBLIÈRE

iUniverse, Inc.
New York   Bloomington

iUniverse books may be ordered through booksellers or by contacting:

iUniverse
1663 Liberty Drive
Bloomington, IN 47403
www.iuniverse.com
1-800-Authors (1-800-288-4677)

Information contained in this handbook was accurate as of the date of publication. Because of the dynamic nature of the Internet, any Web addresses or links contained in this book may have changed since publication and may no longer be valid. The views expressed in this work are solely those of the author and do not necessarily reflect the views of the publisher, and the publisher hereby disclaims any responsibility for them.

ISBN: 978-1-4502-4505-0 (sc)
ISBN: 978-1-4502-4506-7 (ebook)

Printed in the United States of America

iUniverse rev. date: 08/10/2010

Table of Contents

Chapter 1

Introduction

Since 2005, the Government of Canada mantra has been, "Deliver services smarter, faster and at a reduced cost." Accomplishing this means increasing the volume of business that government does with small and medium-sized business owners. The federal government already contracts considerable professional services to supplement the work being done by employees. It will likely do more of that as greater numbers of baby boomers retire from public service.

Industry Canada defines a small business as one with fewer than 100 employees, and a medium-sized business as one with less than 500 staff members.

Micro-businesses—those with only one to four employees—make up a huge proportion of all Canadian businesses. While about 98 per cent of the more than 2.3 million business establishments in Canada can be labelled as either a small or medium-sized firm, a full 57 per cent are micro-businesses.

This handbook is for the little guy. Specifically, for sole proprietors and other micro-businesses offering professional services that could assist the Government of Canada: informatics experts, auditors, business consultants, trainers, writers, editors, translators and others. Micro-businesses are tasked with doing everything to keep their companies afloat, including finding new clients and writing proposals. Yet they have no sales staff and little free time to research a mystifying government procurement process, a process that the Government of Canada vowed in its 2008 Speech from the Throne to make a top priority to fix.

I, too, was once baffled as to how to get contract work with the Canadian government, despite having lived in Ottawa for decades. But after scouring government Web sites and publications, attending business seminars and responding to government tenders, I finally won standing offer awards for English editing and writing services with four federal government departments/agencies. The majority of information in this handbook is publicly available from government Web sites and

1

reports. Hopefully this handbook will save you some legwork as you head down the path toward federal government work.

I welcome all feedback and suggestions for improvements. Please send your comments to info@meseditingandwriting.com.

Marion Soublière
M.E.S. Editing and Writing Services
www.meseditingandwriting.com

Tip

Need contact info for a federal employee? Search the Government Electronic Directory Services (sage-geds.tpsgc-pwgsc.gc.ca).

Chapter 2

How the Federal Government Shops

A $20-billion annual market

Each year, the Canadian government spends about $20 billion on goods and services.

That's for everything from paper clips to tanks to professional services. This last category applies to all kinds of professionals: project managers, auditors, human resources consultants, programmer and systems analysts, application developers, writers, editors, architects, engineers, scientists, translators, researchers, technical support staff, benefits consultants, financial analysts, instructors, change management specialists, and many, many others.

It's the role of Public Works and Government Services Canada (PWGSC) to shop on behalf of the Government of Canada, and in fact it does about 85 per cent of all the shopping—especially for goods. PWGSC buys on behalf of more than 100 departments and agencies, spending about $14 billion yearly on roughly 60,000 transactions. According to PWGSC's 2010-2011 *Report on Plans and Priorities*, PWGSC spending reached a peak of about $18 billion in 2008-2009, with major military purchases spurring the bulk of the increase.

The majority of high-dollar federal contracts emanate from the National Capital Region. PWGSC also lends departments and agencies its spending savvy and expertise when they do their own shopping. Many departments and agencies buy services directly. PWGSC buys only about 18 per cent of the services required by its client departments and agencies.

In 2005, the federal budget introduced fundamental changes to help the Canadian government deliver its services smarter, faster and at a reduced cost, while showing improved accountability. It would spend taxpayers' money more efficiently by increasing the volume of business done with small and medium-sized companies. The Government of Canada has to consider other factors as well when settling on a purchase, including government legislation and rules, internal and international trade agreements, environmental responsibility, socio-economic benefits, and accessibility for Aboriginal companies.

Tip

A key Web site not to be missed is Contracts Canada's site (www.contractscanada.gc.ca), completely revamped as of April 2010.

Delivering services smarter, faster and at a reduced cost hinged on leaving behind the fractured department-by-department habit of buying, and adopting a government-wide procurement approach that consolidates the purchasing requirements of departments. An ambitious PWGSC procurement transformation strategy emphasized ever-greater use of electronic tendering and a few key electronic supplier databases to modernize and streamline procurement. Another change adopted to achieve greater economies of scale was to compel federal buyers to use existing standing offers in the 10 categories of most commonly purchased goods and services:

- ground effect vehicles, motor vehicles, trailers and cycles
- telecommunications equipment and accessories
- general purpose automatic data processing equipment (including firmware), software, supplies and support equipment
- furniture
- office machines, text processing systems and visible recording equipment
- office supplies and devices
- clothing, accessories and insignia
- fuels, lubricants, oils and waxes
- information processing and related telecommunications services, and
- professional, administrative and management support services.

The aim was to get federal buyers to use such standing offers 100 per cent of the time, instead of the more dismal 40 per cent track record. But achieving sweeping changes in procurement while continuing to get the necessary shopping done takes time. PWGSC is still striving to achieve goals such as the enforced use of mandatory standing offers.

While government outreach on federal procurement intensified throughout 2009-2010 with much-improved Web sites and greater numbers of public seminars offered, businesses continued to vent their frustration with the procurement process, red tape and difficulty in finding information about contract opportunities.

During the first half of 2009, a study by the House of Commons Standing Committee on Government Operations and Estimates that originally intended to focus just on the bundling of information technology contracts quickly morphed into something much broader—a set of five public hearings about the challenges bedevilling small and medium-sized companies as they try to compete for federal government contracts.

The committee's report, *In Pursuit of Balance: Assisting small and medium enterprises in accessing federal procurement* (June 2009), made numerous recommendations for improving federal procurement processes. The government's October 19, 2009 report responding to the committee's recommendations pointed out strides made, such as staging regular free seminars across the country to advise suppliers how to conduct business with the government. Another improvement underway was the creation of a single-window Web portal for both Canadian businesses and government buyers that would tell companies how and what to sell to the government. (The site's address, it has since been disclosed, will be www.buyandsell.gc.ca.) Both the committee's and the government's reports can be found at **tinyurl.com/HoC-committees**.

One of the most interesting revelations from the government's report was that the Government of Canada is investigating the possibility of increasing the directed contracting limits for service contracts from $25,000 to $76,500. The $25,000 limit for non-competitive (sole-sourced) contracts "has not changed in over twenty years," stated the government's report. Having the chance to look into raising the limit to $76,500 "will allow the Government to determine if this could improve access for (small and medium-sized enterprises) and reduce the cost of doing business with the government on lower dollar value service contracts."

Businesses know first-hand how discouraging the federal procurement process can be. But it's important to realize that many hard-working federal civil servants are fed up with it, too.

"We received comments from suppliers doing or seeking to do business with the federal government, who were frustrated by government processes and approaches," wrote Procurement Ombudsman Shahid Minto in the first annual report from the new Office of the Procurement Ombudsman, the 2008-2009 report. "In seeking to assist them, our Office found that federal program managers were also frustrated by procurement processes that are complex and slow."

Using the Internet to level the playing field

Harnessing the power of the Internet helps put smaller companies on a level playing field with larger competitors. One of the biggest improvements made in this area was the Canadian government's 2005 decision to drop the fees once required to obtain federal government tenders on MERX (**www.merx.com**), the Internet-based tendering system for most federal government contracts valued at or above $25,000 ($10,000 for printing). For most goods and services below this threshold, PWGSC and departments/agencies seek competitive bids from companies registered on source lists. You'll read more about source lists in Chapter 4, "Where to Look for Contracts."

In 2005, PWGSC also created a new Office of Small and Medium Enterprises (**tinyurl.com/Office-of-SME**), whose raison d'être is to help firms pitch their wares to the federal government. It offers training sessions to businesspeople, as well as presentations to suppliers and industry associations, seeking their suggestions on best practices in procurement. A key component of the Office of Small and Medium Enterprises is Contracts Canada, and these two entities are the prime agencies geared to helping small businesses. (A brief time-out here to clear up any confusion over the name of Contracts Canada: the agency has gone back to this name after being known as Business Access Canada for a few years. Should you see any government Web sites or publications refer to Business Access Canada, be aware that they're talking about Contracts Canada.)

Contracts Canada's Web site (**www.contractscanada.gc.ca**) was completely revamped as of April 2010, and prospective suppliers would be wise to scour every single page of this pivotal site.

Here, businesses can:

- register with the Supplier Registration Information service in order to sell to the government

- find contact info for key government buyers

- get tips for writing a better proposal

- check out times and locations of business seminars across Canada

- scan a database of contracts awarded by PWGSC, and more.

Standing offers, supply arrangements and other purchasing methods

First—a primer on government terms.

Tender: This is the solicitation document that the government publishes to announce that it wants to buy goods or services.

Bid: This is the proposal that you, the potential supplier, submit in response to a tender.

Standing Offer: This is awarded to qualified suppliers who handle some of the government's simpler, more popular needs. These suppliers offer to provide goods and/or services at pre-arranged prices under set terms and conditions on an as-needed basis, and for a limited time only. Standing offers save the government time and money. Once a standing offer has been awarded, the set terms and conditions cannot be further negotiated. The government also has the option to renew the standing offer for several successive years. However, a standing offer is not a contract and the government is not obliged to give you business. No contract exists until the government issues an order against the standing offer, better known as a "call-up."

Request for Standing Offer (RFSO): The government has to solicit bids in order to create a list of standing offer holders, and that's where an RFSO comes in. It details the requirement, bid evaluation method and selection criteria, call-up procedure, ranking methodology (whenever applicable), and all terms and conditions applied to any resulting contract.

Call-up against a Standing Offer: This is a requisition created by a client department to buy goods or services from a supplier who holds a standing offer.

Supply Arrangement: A supply arrangement is another way client departments can solicit bids on specific requirements. A supply arrangement is a list of pre-screened, pre-qualified vendors. Again, the government is not obliged to make a purchase. With supply arrangements, not all terms and conditions are pre-determined (as with standing offers). Many supply arrangements include ceiling prices that let departments negotiate the price down, based on the scope of work.

Request for Proposal (RFP): An RFP is usually used for one-off jobs valued at $25,000 or more, or when the selection of a supplier cannot be made based solely on the lowest price.

Advance Contract Award Notice (ACAN): In this case, a department or agency posts a notice for at least 15 calendar days to inform suppliers that it intends to award a good, service or construction contract to a pre-identified contractor. An ACAN can be challenged, though. If you feel your company can do the work, you can submit a statement of capabilities for the requirement during the 15-day notice period. If your statement meets the requirements, the contracting officer will then proceed with a full tendering process.

Tip

Federal buyers are supposed to rotate through supplier names on a standing offer list so that everyone gets a fair shot at work.

Now that you have the lingo down pat, here is a broad overview of the government shopping process.

Departments and agencies can buy up to $25,000 worth of goods—above that limit, PWGSC must do the shopping for them. For services, departments and agencies are allowed to buy up to $2 million worth of services in many cases.

Crown corporations contract for services on their own and have more flexible procedures than departments.

The federal government usually seeks quotes from different suppliers before making a decision to buy goods or services. Only occasionally does PWGSC follow a non-competitive route to sole-source a contract to a supplier.

PWGSC gets quotes from competitors either through:

- traditional invitations, or

- open bidding on **www.merx.com**.

Traditional invitations are invitations that PWGSC issues to certain bidders for goods and services under $25,000: either a request for quotation with a straightforward bid document, or a telephone buy, in which PWGSC gets at least three quotes over the phone and awards the job to the lowest bid that fulfils all the terms of the job. While an invitation to tender is for purchases above $25,000, it's usually for straightforward off-the-shelf goods. Again, it goes to the lowest bid that fulfils all the mandatory requirements of the job.

Open bidding means that anyone can bid on the government tender. It will be advertised on **www.merx.com**. Suppliers will be responding to either an RFP, an RFSO or a request for supply arrangement. MERX advertises requirements for most goods and services at or above $25,000 ($10,000 for printing). When PWGSC receives bids on government tenders, it works together with departments to evaluate the bids based on pre-determined criteria.

There is a maximum dollar value for call-ups under standing offer periods. (A period is often a year for renewal terms but sometimes the initial period may be shorter or longer, depending on how far away the fiscal year-end is from the time the standing offer is awarded).

For example, the limit on call-ups I get for English editing services for one of my standing offers is $50,000. For another, it's $36,000. But believe me, that doesn't mean I rake in $86,000 from these two standing offers! Remember, federal departments and agencies are not obligated to give you any work if you've been awarded a standing offer.

That's why it's important to continually pitch your expertise to potential buyers (see Chapter 7, "Marketing Yourself.")

Lastly, there are numerous trade agreements and laws that may affect the development of a contract. Read about them and other rules affecting government purchasing in "Step 1: Understand the Process" from *Your Guide to Doing Business with the Government of Canada* (**tinyurl.com/Doing-Business-with-GoC**), published in October 2009 by the Office of Small and Medium Enterprises. It's available in English and French.

Chapter 3

First, Answers to Common Questions

Since publishing the first edition of this handbook in March 2009, I've encountered some basic recurring questions from small businesses related to their eligibility to even consider pursuing federal government work. Let's address those questions here and lay certain doubts to rest.

Do I need to be bilingual to be a federal government supplier?
No, unless the tender you are bidding on contains bilingualism requirements. In the communications field, for example, many standing offers call for English-only writers and editors, and French-only writers and editors. However, one instance where not being bilingual becomes more of an impediment is when you go after on-site contract opportunities through temporary staffing agencies. Most opportunities through temp agencies are for on-site assignments and many require some level of bilingualism.

Does my business need to be located in Ottawa?
No. Although a lot of federal government spending takes place in the National Capital Region, federal departments and agencies have offices throughout Canada. These offices buy services and goods locally. PWGSC regional offices handle many of the department's shopping requirements that are below $25,000. Staff at regional PWGSC offices and regional federal economic development agencies can help you locate contract opportunities. (And consider bidding on a tender whose region of delivery is the National Capital if you can meet the requirements – such as attending meetings in person.) To learn more, check out Chapter 4, "Where to Look for Contracts."

Do I need to be incorporated to be a federal government supplier?
No. The Government of Canada does business with sole proprietors, partnerships, corporations—all kinds of differently structured businesses.

Do I need to be a Canadian citizen to be a federal government supplier?
No, not always. Through the North American Free Trade Agreement
(NAFTA), the World Trade Organization on Government Procurement
and other trade agreements, businesses in the United States, Mexico,
Chile, South Korea and other countries can bid on certain types of
Canadian federal tenders. Read more at Contracts Canada's Web page
on "Trade Agreements" (**tinyurl.com/trade-agreements**).

Tip

The Canadian government considers
everything up to $25,000 to be a low-
dollar buy.

Chapter 4

Where to Look for Contracts

MERX

Canada's main electronic tendering service is the Web site **www.merx. com**, the most complete source of public sector contract opportunities (tenders) in the country—and since 2005, the source of free Government of Canada tender documents.

On MERX, you'll find tenders geared to all kinds of businesses, from sole proprietorships to large corporations. Today, more than 50,000 suppliers use the portal, where more than 1,500 Canadian sales opportunities are open at any particular time.

Established in 1997, MERX is operated on behalf of the federal government by a private company called Mediagrif Interactive Technologies Inc. The government generically refers to the tendering site as GETS, the Government Electronic Tendering System. When federal publications and Web sites refer to GETS, they're talking about MERX.

MERX has more than 2,500 buyers. Federal government buyers use MERX mainly for bigger purchases worth $25,000 or more that are subject to any of the trade agreements. Individual departments generally purchase professional services, and they often do so through MERX. Increasingly, opportunities valued at less than $25,000 are also advertised on MERX.

MERX also posts tenders from the governments of Ontario, Saskatchewan, Manitoba, Alberta, Nova Scotia, Prince Edward Island, New Brunswick, Nunavut, and Newfound and Labrador, as well as more than 500 organizations within the municipal, academic, school boards and hospitals (MASH) sector, the private sector and U.S. government agencies. It also offers information on Canadian private-sector construction projects from the pre-design stage through to the start of construction.

(For links to procurement sites for Canadian provincial and territorial governments that do not participate in MERX—namely, Quebec, British Columbia, Yukon and the Northwest Territories—read Chapter 9, "Getting Work with Other Governments.")

MERX has implemented changes so that any business—no matter how small—can easily access lucrative contracting opportunities with the Canadian government. A major improvement was the move in 2005 to drop the fee to download documents describing federal government tenders. Without these documents, you often can't decide whether you want to bid on a tender or not because you need to first read through the full statement of work and mandatory requirements.

> **Tip**
>
> Don't dismiss a multi-million-dollar tender. See how many suppliers are to receive standing offers under it. An individual award could be in your league.

For example, back in 2004, I paid about $40 to download a tender document looking for on-call editing services for the Department of Foreign Affairs. It was not until I was able to read through the full document, however, that I could see this was not something I wanted to bid on. Editors were required to be on-call overnight for extended periods of time—something I wasn't interested in doing while my daughter was still young. After that experience, I didn't check MERX again for years.

A note of caution: if you download documents, they're free. If you acquire documents by e-mail, mail, fax, courier or pick-up, you'll be charged a small fee. The abstract page summarizing the tender, of course, is free.

Today, a basic subscription to MERX costs nothing. In fact, it's no longer even necessary to use a credit card to subscribe if you only plan on accessing free Government of Canada tender information. (In that case, you would need to register using your Procurement Business Number instead. Read Chapter 5, "Getting Started," to learn how to obtain a Procurement Business Number.)

MERX's basic subscription also includes features such as automatic amendment updates to advise suppliers who have downloaded tenders of possible changes, such as new deadlines. Everyone who downloads a tender is registered in the Document Request List. This is another plus because it shows you who the competition is and may also reveal partnering opportunities.

Beware—don't think that someone who forwards you a solicitation document they obtained as a paying MERX customer is doing you a favour. You *must* order tender solicitation documents directly so that your company's contact information shows up on the Document Request List. Why? Because many buyers disqualify bids that come in from suppliers who aren't on the Document Request List.

Even with a free basic subscription, be sure to log in each time to access all MERX features available to you, such as additional search functions, announcements and more.

All suppliers will automatically receive all questions that businesses send the tender's contracting authority, as well as the contracting authority's answers. This can be very educational, raising points you hadn't yet considered while drafting your proposal. After a tender has closed, you can check back with MERX to see who was awarded standing offers, contracts and so on. Not all departments and agencies disclose that information.

Here's how MERX describes its basic tenders subscription package:

- access to all open opportunity notices of Canadian public-sector buying organizations
- access to all former opportunities and award notices of Canadian public sector buying organizations
- access to international opportunities and government business opportunities
- access to Government of Canada tender documents only. Pay an "out of jurisdiction fee" to access non-federal tender documents ($39.95/order basket for all other Canadian and public sector tenders)
- access to the Document Request List (Government of Canada opportunities only)

- unlimited preview and download of Government of Canada tender documents
- free notification of amendments or cancellations
- one free Opportunity Matching Profile
- free delivery of Opportunity Matching results (e-mail, fax or online).

Or, for $16.95/month, you can subscribe to MERX's complete Canadian public tenders subscription package. It includes everything in the basic package plus:

- access to tender documents from all jurisdictions/regions (federal, provincial and municipal)
- access to all Document Request lists (Canadian opportunities only)
- unlimited preview and download of all tender documents
- free notification of amendments
- free automatic delivery of amendments.

Private tender documents are $25/opportunity. MERX also offers assorted enhanced services, such as the chance to order extra Opportunity Matching profiles and more.

It's important to check MERX every day. It only takes a few minutes. The tendering cycles for some opportunities may last just a few days although, usually, opportunities are posted for a number of weeks. RFSOs for various professional services may only surface every three to four years from federal departments. You don't want to miss a window of opportunity while it's open.

As an editor/writer, I usually check the "Communications, Photographic, Mapping, Printing and Publication Services" and "Professional, Administrative and Management Support Services" categories first thing each morning. There are 52 business categories to choose from overall.

You can also enter key words into the Search function. For best results, use quotation marks around your key words, as well as search operators like "AND," "OR," "NOT" and more. For example: "systems analysis OR application development." Check out a detailed chart with more nifty search operator suggestions in the MERX supplier guide, which you can download from the "Contact Us" page (**tinyurl.com/ MERX-contact**).

When surveying search results before deciding whether or not to proceed to the tender's abstract page, keep a few other tips in mind.

First, one of the categories describing the tender is the region of delivery. For tenders with national delivery, the description often used is "Canada-wide." Sometimes, however, instead of saying "Canada-wide," this category lists every province and territory from coast to coast. The column displays just the first two provinces ("Newfoundland and Labrador, Prince Edward Island, . . ."), which could lead you to think that this tender is for the Atlantic region only. Not so.

Secondly, the title of the tender in the search result may be vague, or inconsistent with wording used in similar tenders. "Review Services," for example, doesn't tell you whether this tender needs financial auditors, business project reviewers, or some other specialty. Don't overlook an opportunity that may be a perfect fit for your skills set.

Another treasure-trove of data can be found when you search for "request for information" or "letter of interest." The federal government sometimes posts such documents months in advance of an actual tender for a variety of reasons. It could be that a department is requesting that suppliers provide information for certain services or goods available so that the department can fashion the most realistic solicitation document possible. It may be a request for consultants to submit expressions of interest for inclusion on a list of potential suppliers to meet future needs or in advance of a tender to be published. Or, it might be a head's up to certain industries that a new procurement opportunity is on its way so that potential bidders can start applying for the appropriate government security clearance immediately. The buyer might even provide contact information to help suppliers get the process started.

MERX underwent a major overhaul in 2009. Take the time to thoroughly learn about all aspects of the new site. Start with the tutorial about public tenders on the home page. It will show you how to search for opportunities, how to order documents, and how to manage and run what they call your "Opportunity Matching Profile" (here, you receive notifications of tenders that match a profile you have created containing your own criteria for opportunities).

MERX also has a handy 21-page supplier guide that explains the newly redesigned site with regard to public tenders, Frequently Asked Questions sections that answer both public and private tender queries, and a glossary of procurement terms. The easiest way to locate all of these is to go to the "Contact Us" page and click on the links there (**tinyurl.com/MERX-contact**). While exploring tenders, you can also click on the "Help" button at the top of each page for more detailed explanations.

For more help, phone MERX at 1-800-964-6379 or (613) 727-4900, Monday to Friday from 7 a.m. to 8 p. m. Eastern Standard Time, fax 1-888-235-5800, or e-mail merx@merx.com (for private tenders, e-mail priv@merx.com). You can also fill out an online support form that goes to customer support. You'll find it on the "Contact Us" page.

Office of Small and Medium Enterprises

One of your first calls should be to the Office of Small and Medium Enterprises, where staff can advise you on you how your goods or services are purchased. Find contact information for regional staff in Chapter 5, "Getting Started."

PWGSC procurement officers and regional staff

The other person who will be at the top of your "must call" list is the procurement officer(s) within PWGSC responsible for the type of good or service you provide. Procurement officers can alert you to business opportunities working their way through the system, which departments have a budget for your commodity, and who the right departmental materiel managers are for you to contact. Consult Contracts Canada's Procurement Allocation Directory to locate PWGSC procurement officers, and the goods and services they buy (**tinyurl.com/PAD-Gov-Canada**).

Staff at PWGSC regional offices across Canada can also tell you about selling opportunities in your area. Click on the multi-coloured map of Canada on the home page of the Contracts Canada site to learn more and to get detailed contact information (**www.contractscanada.**

gc.ca). The site lists the top-spending federal departments/agencies that PWGSC shops for, by province/territory.

Tip

Even with a free MERX basic subscription, be sure to log in each time to access all features available to you.

Nova Scotia
The main buyers are the Department of National Defence, Fisheries and Oceans Canada, and Natural Resources Canada.

New Brunswick and Prince Edward Island
The main buyers are the Department of National Defence, Correctional Service of Canada, and Fisheries and Oceans Canada.

Newfoundland
The main buyers are the Department of National Defence, Fisheries and Oceans Canada, and the National Research Council.

Eastern Quebec (everything east of the Sherbrooke-Trois Rivières axis)
The main buyers are PWGSC, the Department of National Defence, Fisheries and Oceans Canada, and Correctional Service of Canada.

Western Quebec (everything west of the Sherbrooke-Trois Rivières axis, as well as Quebec's northern region)
The main buyers are PWGSC, Correctional Service of Canada, the Department of National Defence, and the Canadian Space Agency.

National Capital Area
Since the Ottawa area is headquarters to the Government of Canada and the lion's share of federal spending takes place here, consider all federal departments and agencies as potential buyers. Suppliers should locate their appropriate purchasing contact in the Procurement Allocations

Directory at **tinyurl.com/PAD-Gov-Canada** (click on "Organizations" in the menu on the left side of the screen).

Ontario (outside the National Capital Area)
The main buyers are the Department of National Defence, Environment Canada, Correctional Service of Canada, and Transport Canada.

Manitoba, Saskatchewan, Alberta, Northwest Territories and Nunavut
PWGSC's Western Region office, which is divided into three regional sectors, doesn't list top federal buyers. Instead, this region says that each sector "works closely with local organizations such as chambers of commerce, municipal purchasing organizations, provincial governments and agencies to provide more business opportunities for Western suppliers."

British Columbia
The main buyers are the Department of National Defence, Fisheries and Oceans Canada, Correctional Service of Canada, Canadian Food Inspection Agency, Agriculture and Agri-Food Canada, and Natural Resources Canada.

Yukon
The main buyers are the Royal Canadian Mounted Police, Parks Canada Agency, PWGSC, the Department of National Defence, and Fisheries and Oceans Canada.

Departmental materiel managers and managers in your field

For contracts under $25,000—or $10,000 for printing—PWGSC turns to source lists for potential suppliers. Departments send PWGSC a list of suggested sources when they submit a requisition for goods or services. And as mentioned earlier, many of the below-$25,000 requirements that PWGSC buys are handled by its regional offices. Getting to know the federal departmental materiel managers and managers in your field (be it communications, IT, human resources, or another area) could land you on a source list. And that will boost your chances of getting contracts.

Materiel managers are responsible for identifying their department's requirements, forwarding requisitions to PWGSC and figuring out specifications. You can view an extensive list of departmental materiel managers across Canada, along with their contact information, at the Contracts Canada Web site (**tinyurl.com/materiel-managers**). Before contacting materiel managers from departments of particular interest to you, make sure the managers' contact information is still up-to-date by cross-referencing it with their listings in the government's online staff directory (**sage-geds.tpsgc-pwgsc.gc.ca**). The Government Electronic Directory Services (GEDS) is regularly updated. Given that there is constant staff movement in the federal public service, spare yourself any wasted efforts by confirming you have the most recent e-mail addresses and phone numbers first.

Using GEDS, you can also track down pertinent departmental managers in your field. For example, as an editor and writer, I would want to touch base with communications directors to determine their needs. When you click on "Department Listing" in the left-hand navigation column on the GEDS site, you get a break-down of each department's organizational structure and contact info for personnel.

As a courtesy, you should e-mail departmental managers rather than phone them. They're busy, and dealing with suppliers is not part of their job description, as is the case with materiel managers.

If, down the road, you are asked to bid on an opportunity, remember that you don't have to say "yes" if you're too busy—but make sure that you respond and explain why you're declining to submit a bid. Otherwise, your name might get removed from the source list.

Regional federal economic development agencies

Staff at regional federal economic development agencies will also help you pinpoint contract opportunities. In some cases, they may point you towards funding to help cover the cost of preparing bids and other procurement activities. For more information, go to Contracts Canada's "Other Federal Programs" Web page (**tinyurl.com/other-federal-programs**).

Atlantic Canada
Atlantic Canada Opportunities Agency (**www.acoa.ca**)

Quebec
Canada Economic Development for Quebec Regions
(**tinyurl.com/Cda-Ec-Dev-Quebec**)

Northern Ontario
Fed Nor (**tinyurl.com/Northern-Ontario**)

Western Canada
Department of Western Economic Diversification
(**tinyurl.com/Western-Cda-Ec-Dev**)

Northern Canada
Canadian Northern Economic Development Agency
(**www.CanNor.gc.ca**)

Firms that already have contracts / Temp agencies

Subcontracting with companies that already have federal government
contracts is a business tactic that the federal government strongly
recommends. To learn about research tools that will unveil companies
with government contracts, or that are standing offer or supply
arrangement holders, read the section about subcontracting with other
companies in Chapter 7, "Marketing Yourself."

You can also work for the Government of Canada via a temp agency.
Glancing at procurement-related government Web pages, one would
never know just how enormous the role of temporary staffing agencies
is these days in terms of carrying out government contracting in the
National Capital Region.

In January 2009, CBC Ottawa reported that spending on temporary
employees in the National Capital Region had almost tripled in the past
five years, rising from $105 million in 2003-2004 to $276 million in
2007-2008. For a government striving to deliver goods and services
more cost-effectively, this is troubling. About 20 per cent of the costs—

or $55.2 million—went towards commissions paid out to temporary agencies.

The federal government says it uses temporary help firms to find temporary staff when a public servant is absent for a period of time, when additional staff are needed during a workload increase, when there aren't enough public servants available to meet the requirement, or when a position is vacant and staffing action is underway.

The Public Service Alliance of Canada (PSAC), the union representing 172,000 federal public servants, disagrees. It has urged the government to discontinue the use of private temporary help agencies.

"These are not temporary positions that are being staffed through employment agencies," Ed Cashman, former regional vice president for the National Capital Region, said in the Summer 2008 PSAC newsletter, *Our Union Voice*.

Still, all signs point toward an ever-escalating use of private temp agencies by the Canadian government. In April 2009, PWGSC awarded standing offers and supply arrangements under a new Temporary Help Services (THS) On-Line System procurement vehicle to 125 companies, to meet the needs of federal departments in the National Capital Region. The government uses the new THS database to find temps for contracts valued at up to $400,000 or lasting 48 consecutive weeks, whichever comes first (previously, the dollar limit was $89,000).

The new THS system has five streams of work: office support, administrative services, operational services, technical services and professional services. These encompass 331 different classifications. The supply arrangement is a new feature. It is typically used for the more complex technical and professional services streams, but can be used for any stream.

According to a May 1, 2009 *Ottawa Citizen* article, inclusion of the supply arrangement "was aimed at addressing complaints that departments were always forced to select the cheapest rather than the best fit or most qualified for the job. The supply arrangement is supposed to give departments flexibility to pick candidates offering the best value for the money."

Clearly, the federal government needs skilled help. And until modern procurement practices are fully up and running, it seems that the government will continue to rely on temp agencies. You might as well take advantage of this. What's more, if you've had a standing offer with a department or agency that has now lapsed, a temp agency that currently has a standing offer with that department or agency will be pleased to learn of your experience. You'll be a good candidate (or "resource," as the government says) for their own standing offer.

The drawback to temp agencies is that they take a cut of your pay (that 20 per cent commission) and may require that you not work directly for a client they've contracted you with for a period of time. On the plus side, the volume of hours you get through a contract might make up for having to share your fee.

Tip

If a federal buyer invites you to bid on work but you're too busy, be sure to at least respond. If not, you might get removed from the source list.

Another drawback is that the vast majority of contracts are for on-site work. Off-site contracts are few and far between. Many client-driven businesses, including one-man shops, need to operate on their own premises in order to tend to their regular stable of clients. Have patience. The stars may eventually align, bestowing a suitable contract upon you.

Detailed contact information for all 125 companies that hold awards for the National Capital Region under the new THS system appears in Appendix A at the end of this handbook. You can register for free with any number of them. While the THS system delivers services to the National Capital Region, sometimes off-site opportunities arise in which the temp agency is looking for qualified suppliers based anywhere who can provide the services remotely.

A number of these agencies also have offices elsewhere in Canada and may hold standing offer awards for temporary help services in other provinces or territories. The Government of Canada has temporary services regional arrangements across the country (Atlantic, Ontario, Pacific, Quebec and Western regions). Search on the "Awards" function on **www.merx.com** to see which temp agencies hold federal standing offers in your region. It's also informative to check agencies' Web sites. Sometimes they spell out all the standing offers / supply arrangements they hold with the federal government, including those for other procurement vehicles.

House of Commons and Senate

The House of Commons and the Senate advertise some, but not all, of their needs on MERX—nor do they have to, because they're not subject to NAFTA.

To land work with the House of Commons and the Senate, you should also enquire about getting your company onto source lists before contracts come up. These are source lists for Parliament's contracting department as well as other divisions, such as its human resources department.

To see if you could be added to the contracting department's source list, contact:

Tamara Taylor
Strategic Procurement Advisor
Materiel and Contract Management
House of Commons
131 Queen St.
Ottawa ON K1A 0A6
Phone: (613) 996-7919
E-mail: TayloT@parl.gc.ca

To be added to source lists for other divisions within Parliament, check **www.parl.gc.ca** or GEDS (**sage-geds.tpsgc-pwgsc.gc.ca**) for contact information. Send your résumé and, ideally, a brochure or marketing piece on your company, with links to your Web site. (Everybody should have a Web site. See Chapter 7, "Marketing Yourself.")

Getting contract work with Members of Parliament (MPs) and Senators is a little different. Funds for contracts may come out of their own budgets, or they may come from a Parliamentary budget. Contact MPs and Senators individually—especially those in your own riding—to see if they would add you to their supplier source lists.

Contact info for Canada's 307 MPs: **tinyurl.com/Members-of-Parliament**.

Contact info for Canada's 104 Senators: **tinyurl.com/Senators-Canada**.

Chapter 5

Getting Started

The Supplier Registration Information service and the all-important Procurement Business Number

The very first thing that all potential suppliers to the Government of Canada should do is register in the Supplier Registration Information (SRI) service (**tinyurl.com/Supplier-Registration**). All you need is your Canada Revenue Agency Business Number and about an hour of time. This will add your company profile to a database of more than 110,000 businesses.

The SRI service, launched in September 1999, was created to become the federal government central registration system for companies wanting to do business with the government.

Prior to the introduction of the SRI service, suppliers had to register in assorted databases maintained by different federal departments or organizations. But databases are becoming consolidated these days in the government's attempt to buy goods and services more efficiently, and the SRI service is the definitive database. In fact, PWGSC won't buy from you unless you're registered with the SRI service. And increasingly, other federal government departments are doing the same.

Unlike other existing departmental vendor databases, your information in SRI is available to all federal government buyers, administrators and employees through the Supplier Information service section of the Contracts Canada Web site (**www.contractscanada. gc.ca**). This information is used for purchasing and invoicing purposes only. Suppliers can only access their own information.

The key benefit that you immediately obtain from the SRI service is the all-important Procurement Business Number (PBN), which identifies a branch, division or office of your company. PWGSC and other federal departments use the PBN for their purchasing and payment systems as a supplier identifier code. You'll need the PBN to register in vendor databases such as Professional Services Online.

The PBN is created using your Canada Revenue Agency Business Number. The Canada Revenue Agency Business Number could be your Goods and Services Tax (GST) or Harmonized Sales Tax (HST) number. Or not. You can have a Canada Revenue Agency Business Number without having a GST/HST. If you don't have a Canada Revenue Agency Business Number, contact the Canada Revenue Agency at 1-800-959-5525 or register online at **www.cra-arc.gc.ca/bn**.

If you have a GST/HST number, then the PBN consists of the first nine digits of your GST/HST number, plus two letters and four numbers identifying your procurement account.

Tip

Always check for new SRI commodities categories that reflect your services. Most government buyers search the Supplier Information database by commodities.

A word about your company name, if you're in the process of getting your GST/HST number and are still picking a name. If you plan to register your GST/HST number under your company name, take a moment to consider whether that name sounds clear and competent. Sometimes the only information a project authority ends up with on you (despite the 60-page bid you slaved over and submitted for evaluation) is your name, contact info and rates. Canada Business (**www.canadabusiness.ca**), a joint initiative between federal, provincial/territorial and private sector organizations to help businesses access a wider range of information on government services, programs and regulations, offers sage advice when considering how to choose a name.

Registering in the SRI service is a two-step process. Once you provide your GST/HST number, Contracts Canada verifies your number with the Canada Revenue Agency and then furnishes you with a PBN, along with a user name and password to create an account. Then you set up an online account that includes:

- your name, mailing address, phone number and e-mail address

- PBN

- type of ownership (whether a sole proprietorship, corporation, partnership or other entity)

- country of ownership

- your business's operating name

- the number of employees in your business

- your business sector (this identifies who your services are geared to—who most of your clients are)

- the official language you operate in

- whether or not you are an Aboriginal supplier

- commodity information (these are the types of goods or services you provide, chosen from a PWGSC database of hundreds of commodities), and

- comments about your company (here you can briefly list your experience, areas of expertise, types of projects you've worked on, your main clients, your level of security clearance, etc., and link to your Web site).

Keep your PBN, user name and password in a safe place. You'll need these to update your account. You should do this on a regular basis, at least once every quarter. Add new information about your business, and check to see if any new SRI commodities categories have been introduced to the master list. If they reflect services that you offer, add them to your company profile.

While it is possible for government buyers to search records by a supplier's legal or operating name, address, PBN or telephone number, they usually conduct a search by commodities. This is another important reason to keep your SRI profile up-to-date with the latest commodities categories.

Registering in SRI and other databases is just the first step on the way to getting work with the federal government. Being listed doesn't mean that you'll automatically get a contract. You'll need to promote your company and services to contacts in government departments, like the materiel managers, departmental managers and procurement officers mentioned earlier. They may suggest you as a supplier, possibly giving you a chance to bid. You should also register in other supplier databases, described next in this chapter.

Should you need help registering in SRI, contact the regional SRI agent closest to you: **tinyurl.com/SRI-contacts**.

Other supplier databases and procurement vehicles

With the all-important PBN in hand, you can now apply to become registered in other government-wide supplier databases that showcase your area of expertise:

- Professional Services Online
- SELECT
- Task-Based Informatics Professional Services and Solutions-Based Informatics Professional Services
- Cyber Protection Supply Arrangement
- Task-Based and Solutions-Based Professional Services
- In-Service Support Supply Arrangement
- Learning Services
- Professional Audit Support Services
- Translation Bureau, and
- Technical, Engineering and Maintenance Services Supply Arrangement.

With some methods of supply, such as Professional Services Online, SELECT and the Translation Bureau, you can apply any time of the year. For some of the other databases, you can only do so when the supply arrangement or standing offer is being "refreshed" or "re-competed"— meaning, when the list opens up again to accept new suppliers. You'll find notices on **www.merx.com** with the appropriate deadlines. With some databases, work descriptions of job positions have been posted. Be sure to read them to ensure you're not overlooking opportunities that befit your talents.

Most supplier databases, like the SRI service, do not show you what government work is available, the way MERX does. They simply allow you to market your wares. And as with the SRI service, you can't rest on your laurels after being registered. You must promote your company and services to key government contacts.

Professional Services Online

Professional Services Online, better known as PS Online (**tinyurl. com/PS-Online**), is a supply arrangement of approved suppliers offering informatics and non-informatics professional services. Federal departments and agencies can consult this database when they want to award professional services contracts worth up to $76,600. This is the NAFTA threshold.

PS Online is said to be used largely outside the National Capital Region, since anything up to $76,600 is still considered a lower-dollar contract. This makes PS Online a particularly appealing procurement tool for smaller businesses. And unlike some other federal supply arrangements, PS Online does not require businesses to have achieved certain revenues in order to be eligible.

For federal government buyers, one of the advantages of using PS Online is that it shortens the competitive procurement process to a minimum of 10 working days by mail and a minimum of 5 working days by fax. This compares to the 15 to 40 days it takes if using MERX.

Anyone can register on PS Online, even a sole proprietor. Here, you highlight the skills and experience of your employees (even if that's only you), as well as your per diem rates. PS Online supplies a chart of per diem ceiling rates for various job types, based on years of experience. The figures are marketplace-driven. If, for example, there are a lot of suppliers with nine-plus years of experience on a given day, and fewer suppliers with five to eight years of experience, it's possible the more junior supplier could command the higher price on that particular day. The data fluctuate all the time because new suppliers with a varying range of experience are continually being registered with PS Online.

PS Online opened up to areas outside the National Capital Region in May 2006. It replaced an earlier vendor database called the Informatics Professional Services Marketplace. However, PS Online showcases suppliers who offer not only informatics professional services, but non-IT (information technology) professional services as well. There are 26 job categories under the heading of informatics professional services and 41 job categories on the non-IT professional services side.

Tip

Want to know which departments operate in your area? Check Contracts Canada's list of materiel managers by province/territory to find out **(www.contractscanada.gc.ca)**

IT Professional Services	
• Business Transformation Architect	• Programmer Analyst
• Call Centre Consultant	• Project Administrator
• Database Administrator / Analyst	• Project Leader
• Enterprise Architect Consultant	• Project Manager
• Information Architect	• Quality Assurance Consultant
• Internet / Intranet Site Specialist	• Senior Platform Analyst
• IT Project Executive	• Senior Systems Analyst
• IT Risk Management Service	• Systems Auditor
• IT Security Consultant	• Technology Analyst
• IT Technical Writer	• Technology Architect
• IT Tester	• Technology Operator
• Platform Analyst	• Web Accessibility Services
• Programmer	• Wireless Application Services Consultant

PS Online's IT job categories

Non-IT Professional Services

• Benefits Consultant	• Human Resources Policies Specialist
• Business Architect Consultant	• Instructor
• Business Process Transformation Consultant	• Knowledge Management Consultant
• Change Management / Organizational Development Services	• Leadership Development Services
• Classification Design Services	• Needs Analysis Services
• Communication and Information Services	• Organizational Assessment Consultant
• Compensation Analyst	• Organizational Design
• Courseware Developer	• Organizational Design Consultant
• Current Classification Standards (other than Executive Group Evaluation Plan) Work Description Writing	• Organizational Development Services
• Current Classification Standards (other than Executive Group Evaluation Plan) Classification Evaluation and (or) Grievance Committees	• Procurement Specialist
• Employee Relations Advisor	• Project Assistant
• Employment Interviewer	• Project Management Services
• Employment Manager	• Project Manager
• Executive Group Evaluation Plan Classification Evaluation and (or) Grievance Committees	• Research Services
• Executive Group Evaluation Plan Work Description Writing	• Scenario Planning Consultant
• Financial Analyst	• Training and Development Specialist
• Group Facilitator	• Transition Support Services
• Human Resources Assistant	• Virtual Workplace Consultant

PS Online's non-IT job categories

Non-IT Professional Services	
• Human Resources Consultant	• Work Description Writer
• Human Resources Disability and Equity Advisor	• Writer
• Human Resources Information System Specialist	

PS Online's non-IT job categories

Registering on PS Online is more time-consuming than registering with the SRI service. You'll need to mail or fax in some mandatory required information, including a company profile. If you are incorporated, send a copy of your incorporation charter showing the date and place of incorporation. If you aren't incorporated, provide proof of business registration. You must also state the number of years you've been in business, and provide a human resources plan and a detailed description of at least three relevant projects you've carried out in the last three years. See an example from my submission to PS Online on the following page:

Newsletter *(Tukimut 2006)*

Client
Indian and Northern Affairs Canada—
Nunavut Region

Duration of project
November 2005–January 2006

Work completed by M.E.S. Editing and Writing Services
•   Researched and wrote all English text for the office's four-language economic development newsletter, Tukimut 2006, which was distributed in print format throughout Nunavut in March 2006 and is available online at www.ainc-inac.gc.a/nu/nuv/ecd_e.html.

•   Obtained all photos and logos to accompany articles, and arranged to get signed release forms of individuals featured in the photos.

•   Secured feedback on articles from program clients before publication.

•   Provided design advice to the INAC editor and additional editorial insight gleaned from doing interviews.

HOW CHALLENGES WERE MET: Time lines were tight for this project—just three weeks to set up and conduct interviews, do additional research, write stories and provide draft text to client. Pinning sources down for interviews is a time-consuming process in northern Canada because people may be travelling (which can only be done by plane and often takes the better part of a week) or out on the land hunting. Despite the schedule, M.E.S. Editing and Writing Services met all client deadlines for deliverables. The INAC—Nunavut Region office reported receiving many positive comments from readers after the print copy of Tukimut 2006 was circulated in March 2006.

Deliverables
1. Ten main articles (approximately 250 words each).
2. Four sidebars (approximately 125 words each).
3. Forty high-resolution colour photos and logos, from which the client eventually selected 21 photos and logos.
4. Fourteen signed photo release forms.
5. Feedback on text from 12 program clients.

Roles performed by M.E.S. Editing and Writing Services:
- Researcher
- Writer
- Editor
- Photo researcher
- Project manager

Sample summary of a work project for PS Online application

You also need to supply signed certifications verifying that the claims made in your mandatory requirements, such as your education, are true. As well, you must review a Trading Partner Agreement, sign the agreement and submit it. For step-by-step instructions to registering on PS Online, go to **tinyurl.com/PS-Online-register**. Allow about three to four weeks for your application to be reviewed.

If your application is approved, then you'll receive a user name and password in order to create an account. This account will ask you to fill in much of the same information as the SRI service account, with a few additional details: your annual revenues, security clearance, whether you have foreign ownership, whether you are Aboriginal-owned, where you conduct business, and your Web site address.

Even if you are a sole proprietor, be sure to fill out a consultant's form for yourself as part of your account. This is where you will indicate your skills and per diem rates. These are all-inclusive ceiling per diem rates (all-inclusive includes displacement costs and GST/HST). Federal government department users can negotiate the price down. For many professionals who come from a private sector background, these rates will look appealingly generous. Here are some examples of ceiling per diem rates as of mid-May 2010:

Summary of Rates (average/year)				
Category	Years of Experience			
	1-2	3-4	5-8	9+
IT Project Executive	$765	$861	$951	$1,064
Human Resources Consultant	$835	$869	$962	$1,130
Writer	$678	$632	$676	$907

Examples of some PS Online ceiling per-diem rates

You can update the information in your account at any time. As a matter of fact, you must go into your account and "refresh" it—or update it—at least once every quarter. Otherwise, your account will be deleted.

You must also submit quarterly activity reports to PWGSC, even if you haven't received any work. If not, your account risks getting the boot. Check PS Online's step-by-step supplier guide for information to include in your report (**tinyurl.com/PS-Online-supplier-guide**). E-mail reports by April 15, July 15, October 15 and January 15 to rcnspenligne.ncrpsonline@tpsgc-pwgsc.gc.ca.

Tip

PS Online is used largely outside the National Capital Region, since anything up to $76,600 is still considered a lower-dollar buy.

Be sure to check the "News Bulletin" section of the PS Online site for important supplier updates (**tinyurl.com/PS-Online-news-bulletins**). This is where you will learn about such things as changes in PS Online rules, or new skills that have been added to the master list that you may want to add to your profile.

If you have a question about PS Online, contact rcnspenligne. ncrpsonline@tpsgc-pwgsc.gc.ca. For technical assistance and help if you've forgotten your password, contact basa-assd@tpsgc-pwgsc.gc.ca.

SELECT

SELECT (**tinyurl.com/SELECT-SA**) is a database for suppliers who provide construction, architectural and engineering services, as well as suppliers who provide related maintenance and consulting services. PWGSC uses SELECT to invite firms to bid on real property opportunities for consulting up to $76,600 and construction up to $100,000.

If you plan to register under construction or maintenance services, you'll need to outline general company information, specific trades for which your firm wishes to apply licence data (if registering for a licensed trade) and reference project data.

If you intend to register under consulting services—which include architecture, engineering or related real property consulting—you'll need to outline general company information, the provinces/territories in which your firm is currently licensed or authorized to practice (corresponding to disciplines), employee qualification information, and project information and employee responsibility on projects.

Send questions about SELECT to the supplier registration agent for your area (**tinyurl.com/SELECT-contact**).

Task-Based Informatics Professional Services and Solutions-Based Informatics Professional Services

PWGSC created the Task-Based Informatics Professional Services supply arrangement, better known as TBIPS (**tinyurl.com/TBIPS**), to help equip the federal government with task-based information management and IT professional services. TBIPS consists of both a standing offer and a supply arrangement. Suppliers handle specific IT tasks that usually are not large projects. In fact, they may be part of larger projects. The projects have an established start date, end date and set deliverables. Assignments may call for unique skills or knowledge, with highly specialized work to be completed in a short period of time.

PWGSC also created a Solutions-Based Informatics Professional Services, or SBIPS (**tinyurl.com/SBIPS**), supply arrangement. TBIPS and SBIPS are becoming the main contracting vehicles for most federal government informatics services requirements. (PS Online is used for lower-dollar informatics contracts.)

SBIPS is refreshed quarterly while TBIPS is refreshed annually to permit new suppliers to qualify and to allow current supply arrangement holders to apply for additional streams and categories. (In government terms, a "stream" is a broad category, and a "category" is a subset of a stream.) To find out how to become a qualified supply arrangement holder, or if you have any other questions about TBIPS or SBIPS, e-mail rcnmdai-ncrimos@tpsgc-pwgsc.gc.ca. For technical assistance, contact basa-assd@tpsgc-pwgsc.gc.ca.

Cyber Protection Supply Arrangement

PWGSC uses the Cyber Protection Supply Arrangement, or CPSA (**tinyurl.com/Cyber-Protection-SA**), to deliver informatics security services on an "as and when requested" basis to federal departments, agencies, Crown corporations and others.

To learn more, browse the detailed Frequently Asked Questions section on the CPSA site. To find out how to be added as a supplier to the CPSA supply arrangement, check **www.merx.com**. The CPSA site lists all current supply arrangement holders.

If you have a question about the CPSA, contact acqbcpsa.dgaamac@ tpsgc-pwgsc.gc.ca.

Task-Based and Solutions-Based Professional Services

PWGSC's newest method of supply provides the federal government with services for business / change management, project management and human resources through 31 job types found within these three broad categories.

The Task-Based and Solutions-Based Professional Services supply method, called TSPS for short (**tinyurl.com/TSPS-tool**), consists of one standing offer for "tasks" and two supply arrangements—one for "tasks" and one for "solutions." Like TBIPS and SBIPS, this new purchasing tool divvies work requirements up into tasks and solutions.

Task-based services fulfil a particular activity with defined responsibilities and expected deliverables. Often, the activity will have a start date and end date. The activity might be part of a larger project, and can be for short or long periods of time. Solutions-based services do not apply to a particular activity. Instead, they are used for larger issues of how to resolve business problems. TSPS is meant to complement existing procurement tools like PS Online.

The TSPS standing offer and supply arrangement for tasks are to be refreshed before the end of the first 15-month initial period of the standing offer and supply arrangement awards handed out in May 2010. After that, TSPS will open up once a year so that new suppliers can qualify and existing suppliers can apply for additional streams. Check **www.merx.com** for notices. Suppliers will be able to find a permanent notice on MERX inviting them to submit proposals for the TSPS supply arrangement for solutions.

At the time of publication, no Web site existed yet for the TSPS method of supply. You can e-mail questions about TSPS to SPTS. TSPS@tpsgc-pwgsc.gc.ca.

In-Service Support Supply Arrangement

The In-Service Support Supply Arrangement, or ISS SA (**tinyurl. com/ISS-Supply**), is a list of approved suppliers for human resource, organizational and project management consulting services. The ISS SA is usually updated each year to permit new suppliers to qualify and to allow current supply arrangement holders to apply for additional streams and categories. The current period of the supply arrangement runs through to September 30, 2010. A notice about the opportunity to get in on the ISS SA will be posted on **www.merx.com** and the ISS SA site.

The ISS SA site also lists the more than 300 existing supply arrangement holders and their contact information. This lets you size up the competition and scope out possible partners or sub-contracting opportunities (**tinyurl.com/ISS-Supply-holders**). And, unlike most other supplier databases, you can check out current contracting opportunities (**tinyurl.com/ISS-Supply-Contracts**).

Learning Services

This standing offer and supply arrangement is used under certain circumstances to create, update or convert government-owned training courses, including training material.

PWGSC will post a notice on **www.merx.com** every two years to allow new suppliers to be added and to allow existing suppliers to apply for additional streams and categories. The current standing offer / supply arrangement period runs until May 31, 2011.

To discover more, check the Frequently Asked Questions portion of the Learning Services site (**tinyurl.com/Learning-Services-SO-SA**), or e-mail ServicesApprentissageOCAMA-LearningServicesSOSA@ tpsgc-pwgsc.gc.ca.

Professional Audit Support Services

The Office of the Comptroller General and PWGSC recently created the Professional Audit Support Services (PASS) supply arrangement in support of the Government of Canada's new *Policy on Internal Audit and/or Internal Control*. PASS is a mandatory supply arrangement for the purchase of audit and financial management services provided on an "as and when requested" basis to federal departments, agencies and Crown corporations. PASS covers eight work streams:

- internal audit services
- practice inspections
- IT and systems audits
- forensic audits
- external audits
- financial and accounting services
- internal control training
- recipient / contribution agreements audits.

PASS is refreshed every 18 months so that new suppliers can qualify and existing supply arrangement holders can apply for additional streams. Check **www.merx.com** for notices. A Web site geared to suppliers is expected to go online in the summer of 2010 but in the meantime, more information about the supply arrangement can be gleaned from this Treasury Board of Canada Secretariat site for federal buyers: **tinyurl.com/PASS-SA**.

If you have a question about the PASS supply arrangement, contact peggy.gilmour@tpsgc-pwgsc.gc.ca.

Tip

Submitting a quote for a call-up may be more urgent than the job itself, with an end-of-day or next-day deadline.

Translation Bureau

The Translation Bureau (**www.btb.gc.ca**) relies on a pool of small and medium-sized linguistic services firms to help it meet increasing demand for translation, revision, interpretation, localization and other services that are delivered to Parliament, the Judiciary and federal departments and agencies in English and French, as well more than 150 Aboriginal and foreign languages. On-call twenty-four hours a day, seven days a week, the Bureau provides services to other governments in Canada and to international organizations, too.

If you are a translator or interpreter, apply to be included in the Bureau's Inventory of Linguistic Service Suppliers (**tinyurl.com/ Linguistic-Suppliers**).

Technical, Engineering and Maintenance Services Supply Arrangement

PWGSC uses this supply arrangement to deliver technical professional services on an "as and when requested" basis. For the Department of National Defence, it's mandatory to use the Technical, Engineering and Maintenance Services supply arrangement, also known as TEMS (**tinyurl.com/TEMS-SA**). Streams of work include general administration services, general engineering and related services, telecommunication services, clothing/textile services and technical support services.

To find out how to be added as a supplier to the TEMS supply arrangement, check **www.merx.com**. There is always a notice on MERX describing the TEMS supply arrangement. The TEMS site also lists all current supply arrangement holders.

If you have a question about the TEMS supply arrangement, contact rcn.aastie-ncr.temssa@tpsgc-pwgsc.gc.ca.

Seminars on doing business with the government

Do yourself a big favour and enrol in a free seminar on doing business with the Government of Canada (**tinyurl.com/OSME-seminars**)— especially before attempting your first proposal.

The Office of Small and Medium Enterprises offer seminars in larger cities across Canada, including Halifax, Quebec City, Montreal, Ottawa/Gatineau, Toronto, Winnipeg, Regina, Saskatoon, Edmonton, Calgary and Vancouver.

Over the past year, the Office of Small and Medium Enterprises has ramped up the number of seminars it offers. It's also partnering with more private and public sector organizations to offer seminars through an increased number of venues and in some smaller towns. For example, in the National Capital Region, the Ottawa Centre for Research and Innovation provides the Office of Small and Medium Enterprises with an additional venue for seminars, in addition to those hosted in the Office of Small and Medium Enterprises' own lodgings in Gatineau. In western and northern Canada, it partners with groups such as the Canadian Manufacturers and Exporters Association, the Province of Alberta, Saskatchewan Economic Development Agencies, the Winnipeg Construction Association, and the Northwest Territories and Nunavut Association of Professional Engineers and Geoscientists to offer seminars in places such as Lethbridge (Alberta), Dauphin (Manitoba) and other more rural or remote locales.

Nonetheless, it's quite possible these seminars won't be coming to a town near you. If that's the case, check out *How to Do Business with the Government of Canada,* a very insightful Webinar produced by TD Canada Trust in August 2009, featuring an interview with the Office of Small and Medium Enterprises' Manny Argiropoulos, chief of small and medium enterprises stakeholder engagement (**tinyurl.com/TD-Canada-Trust-Webinar**).

Occasionally, the Office of Small and Medium Enterprises also teams up with municipal or provincial governments to deliver joint presentations to business audiences, giving them even more value for their investment of time. The Ontario government, for example, was to give a presentation on the province's new HST. In the fall of 2009, the City of Ottawa, keen to find more suppliers to bid on the municipality's own tenders, gave a presentation on how the city's procurement process works.

Federal government seminars are available Canada-wide, although they may differ regionally in terms of structure. It's necessary to take the introductory seminar to enrol in the others. The seminars include:

- **Doing Business with the Government of Canada (introductory seminar):** This seminar describes how the government does its buying, what it buys, how to register your business in supplier registration databases, how to promote yourself and how to find bidding opportunities.

- **Bidding on Opportunities:** This seminar provides advice and guidance on preparing a proposal, on requirements of an RFP, how businesses should respond to an RFP, and how bids are evaluated.

- **Professional Services Online:** This seminar details, step by step, how to register your firm in this automated procurement tool geared to helping federal departments identify IT and non-IT professionals for their lower-dollar value needs.

- **Understanding SELECT:** This seminar explores SELECT, a database of suppliers qualified to perform specialty construction, or architectural and engineering consulting services. PWGSC uses this database to identify potential suppliers for lower-dollar value requirements.

Seminars are generally limited, so it's wise to register early. Check **tinyurl.com/OSME-seminars** for dates and sign up at least two weeks in advance. (Ontario businesses should check for dates and locations of additional seminars on the Office of Small and Medium Enterprises' Ontario Region Web site: **tinyurl.com/OSME-Ontario**.) You can also contact the Office of Small and Medium Enterprises for free advice. National InfoLine: 1-800-811-1148. E-mail: ncr.contractscanada@ tpsgc-pwgsc.gc.ca. In the case of the Ottawa, Toronto and Halifax branches, you can also drop by for an in-person consultation. Phone in advance to book an appointment.

Office of Small and Medium Enterprises Regional Offices

National Capital Region (in-person service from 9 a.m. – 4 p.m., Monday to Friday) Tower OC1-100A Place du Portage 3 11 Laurier St. Gatineau QC K1A 0S5 Toll-free: 1-800-811-1148 E-mail: ncr.osme@pwgsc-tpsgc.gc.ca	Western Region 5th Floor, Telus Plaza North 10025 Jasper Ave. Edmonton AB T5J 1S6 Phone: (780) 497-3801 E-mail: osme-bpme-wst@pwgsc-tpsgc. gc.ca
Ontario Region (in-person service from 8:30 a.m. – 5 p.m., Monday to Friday) 2nd Floor, 4900 Yonge St. Toronto ON M2N 6A6 Toll-free: 1-800-668-5378 Phone: (416) 512-5577 E-mail: ONT.osme-bpme@pwgsc- tpsgc.gc.ca	Quebec Region Suite 7300 Southeast Portal, 800 de la Gauchetière St. W. Montreal QC H5A 1L6 Phone: (514) 496-3525 E-mail: QueBPME.QueOSME@pwgsc- tpsgc.gc.ca
Atlantic Region (in-person service from 8:30 a.m. – 4:30 p.m., Monday to Friday) 236 Brownlow Ave. Dartmouth NS B3B 1V5 Phone: (902) 426-5677 E-mail: osme-bpme-atl@pwgsc-tpsgc. gc.ca	Pacific Region Room 1210, 800 Burrard St. (Mailing: Room 641, 800 Burrard St.) Vancouver BC V6Z 2V8 Toll-free: 1-866-602-0403 Phone: (604) 775-6859 E-mail: osme-bpme-pac@pwgsc-tpsgc. gc.ca

Procurement Strategy for Aboriginal Business: Set-asides

Aboriginal Canadians have been this country's most disenfranchised citizens, sometimes living in socio-economic conditions more commonly found in Third World countries. The federal government created the Procurement Strategy for Aboriginal Business (PSAB) to help level the playing field for Aboriginal entrepreneurs by enabling Aboriginal firms to do more contracting with all federal government departments and agencies.

Under the PSAB, the federal government sets aside certain contracts for competition among Aboriginal businesses. There are two kinds of PSAB set-asides: mandatory and voluntary. A mandatory set-aside policy applies to all contracts over $5,000 that serve a mainly Aboriginal population. Federal buyers may apply voluntary set-asides to other contracts when it's practical to do so. When a contract is reserved for Aboriginal competition, the RFP or advertisement for that contract will state the set-aside requirement.

In Canada, there are three recognized Aboriginal groups: Indians, Inuit and Métis. If your company qualifies as an Aboriginal firm, you should register it in order to pursue Aboriginal procurement set-asides. This Web site (**tinyurl.com/Aboriginal-set-aside-program**) explains the registration process that you'll need to follow.

Tip

A supply arrangement isn't confined to a period of time, like a standing offer. Once you're in, you're in, as long as you continue to qualify.

Chapter 6

Preparing a Winning Proposal

The more proposals you write, the easier it becomes

This is the part most people hate with a passion—writing the proposal.

While the feds are trying to streamline the process (in some cases introducing templates to be filled out instead of asking that a proposal be created from scratch), the reality is that preparing a bid can still be extremely time-consuming.

You could be looking at a week or more in unpaid labour in order to create a technical offer, a financial offer and a compilation of signed certification requirements. The technical offer, by far, will take most of your time. It's here where you must respond precisely to mandatory requirements and point-rated criteria, detailing your expertise and recent projects accomplished, and in some cases, supplying work samples and letters of references.

The most complex standing offer I've responded to featured a 57-page bilingual solicitation document. The standing offer, worth a maximum $18.5 million over a five-year period, was looking for 76 translators, editors and proofreaders. The department issued 16 question-and-answer documents throughout the solicitation period, and held a bidders' conference at its headquarters that drew close to 30 suppliers on-site and perhaps another half dozen participating via teleconference.

The good news is that the more proposals you write, the more you cut and paste from previous bids, and the faster you can respond to the tender. You don't have to reinvent the wheel each time.

While the federal government claims to have simplified the language in the majority of solicitation documents in recent years, many business owners would argue it's still convoluted and unclear at times. That's why attending a government seminar on doing business with the

Government of Canada is vital. They focus, in part, on responding to government tenders.

First-time bidders will also be interested to learn that supplier rates requested for standing offers are not always based on a flat hourly rate. Sometimes, tenders request one hourly rate for regular business hours, a second hourly rate for weekends/evenings, and a third hourly rate for statutory holidays worked. Or different rates may be required for urgent vs. regular work.

The bid evaluation process takes months. Sometimes, many months.

The quickest evaluation of one of my bids was two and a half months. The longest was six and a half months. In that case, the department asked bidders to agree to an extension on the evaluation period, but they did so by mailing bidders a notification of the extension at the end of August, during the dog days of summer. Bidders had to fax or e-mail back their response agreeing to the extension by September 7—unfortunate for anyone on their summer holidays.

Tip

Even if 300 companies are on a MERX Document Request List for a tender, remember that only a handful may end up bidding.

Tips for bidders

- Always read the solicitation document thoroughly. Then have someone else read it as well. Compare notes to ensure everyone is clear on the requirements.

- The mandatory requirements are especially important. If you don't meet all mandatory requirements, your proposal won't even make it to the evaluation stage. Point-rated criteria, meanwhile, are used to assess value-added factors that go beyond the minimum requirements of the solicitation document.

- If you're responding to an RFP, you'll have to lay out a solution to the client's problem, be it constructing an innovative data warehouse or re-energizing an annual report. Describe your plan of attack, why it should be a stellar success, any problems that might arise and how you would mitigate them, and then outline tasks, deliverables and a work schedule, explaining who would be handling which tasks.

- Direct any questions about the tender to the buyer (that's the contracting authority / contracting officer / procurement officer) whose name appears on the first page of the solicitation document. Don't call anyone else in the department that's buying the services. If you do, it presents a conflict of interest and could get your bid thrown out.

- Ask questions well in advance. Your solicitation document will probably state that questions have to be asked within a certain number of days before the closing date. Remember that all questions and answers will be compiled by PWGSC (or the department that's buying the services) and sent to each supplier for their information. Don't give away any trade secrets in your questions, and don't expect government officials to provide you with answers that give you a competitive edge. (Although I do remember one federal department, when asked what average hourly rate was charged by editors under the department's last standing offer, came right out with the figure—$65/hour.)

- You may be asked to provide samples of your work from past projects. If you haven't religiously kept samples over the years, start now—especially samples from federal government projects. The federal government likes to see that you've worked on federal government projects in the past, and often asks for samples from recent projects.

- You can try asking for a deadline extension. Deadlines certainly have been changed before if there is enough demand from bidders. But don't wait until 48 hours prior to the deadline because then it will be too late.

49

- You can also try asking for criteria to be changed. Again, if there is enough demand from bidders, the department may bend. For one of the RFSOs that I responded to, the client originally would only accept work samples from federal government projects. The department changed its policy after enough bidders complained, allowing bidders to submit work samples from projects for other governments and the private sector as well.

- Follow the instructions of the solicitation document to the letter. If you are asked to put the technical, financial and certification requirements into separate envelopes and then put them all into one larger envelope, do it.

- Organize your proposal so that it matches the sequence of the solicitation document. Make your offer complete, concise and precise. You can also mirror some of the exact wording used in the solicitation document. That way, the evaluation team can see you've addressed their requirements. For example, one RFSO that I responded to contained this requirement: "The Bidder must demonstrate its level of technical ability to accept electronic orders; send electronic confirmations; provide electronic status updates; provide electronic account statements." So in my technical offer, I said, "M.E.S. Editing and Writing Services can accept electronic orders, send electronic confirmations, provide electronic status updates and provide electronic account statements via its e-mail address, info@meseditingandwriting.com." We already knew that an e-mail address was the answer they were looking for because it had been a question raised by one of the suppliers earlier and we all received the answer.

- Be on the lookout for the words "must," "shall" and "will"— these indicate that you have to do what is asked, without any deviation.

- Stumped by an acronym you've stumbled across in a solicitation document? Check out this PWGSC glossary: **tinyurl.com/GoC-acronyms**.

- Always make it clear whether you were the contractor or subcontractor on a particular project that you're citing as a work sample. I've been called to task before over this discrepancy.

- Include Web site addresses wherever possible. These may link to online samples of your work, to your clients' Web sites, and so on. Evaluators will definitely check these sites. It makes it easier for them to verify your work and level of professionalism.

- Include colour graphics where you can, particularly to illustrate work that you've done. The government doesn't ask for this but I think visuals make a huge impact. With photo editing software, it's easy to do a screen capture of the home page of that federal government Web site project you worked on recently, convert it into a .jpg, resize it and insert it into your technical offer.

- Include a table of contents, and be sure that your cover page contains any specific information requested by the solicitation document, such as that document's reference number.

- Put your logo or company name on each page so that the bid evaluation team can identify your pages if they take proposals apart to compare similar sections.

- If you don't meet the security requirements outlined in the tender, ask in your bid that the buyer sponsor you.

- If time permits, lay out your technical and financial offers in a desktop publishing program and get your hard copies professionally bound at a quick print shop. Again, this is not a government requirement but I think the visual sleekness of such a document makes a strong impression. I worked for a communications agency for more than a decade and they always, always laid their proposals out in Quark and then coil-bound them.

- Usually bids have to be submitted as hard copies but occasionally now, some government tenders also allow you to e-mail your proposal. The solicitation document will explain whether that is possible and how you should confirm that the e-mail with your attached proposal has been received.

Tip

Don't have all the skills or resources required to bid on a particular tender? Partner up with other businesses to submit a proposal together.

- If submitting hard copies of your proposal, don't wait until minutes before the tender deadline to hand it in. And make sure you deliver it to the right address. The contracting authority's address can be different from the receiving bids division address.

- Not all government departments let you know whether your bid has won or not. If you don't hear back, follow up with the contracting authority. Make sure you give them time to do the bid evaluations first.

- You may be able to find out whose bids won by checking **www.merx.com** (on the home page, click on "Awards" in the drop-down box headed by "Open Opportunities," and enter a search term in the field to the left). You can also see who is getting business by looking through this Treasury Board of Canada Secretariat site (**tinyurl.com/TBS-contracts-awarded**) for all contracts over $10,000 awarded. You could also check Contracts Canada's Contract History section (**tinyurl.com/Contract-History**).

- Finally, win or lose, always ask for a debriefing to find out what could have been improved in your proposal or what was successful. This way, you're also making yourself known to the contracting authority, a good marketing manoeuvre.

For more information about writing effective proposals, read "Step 5: Bid on Opportunities" in the Office of Small and Medium Enterprises'

Your Guide to Doing Business with the Government of Canada (**tinyurl. com/Doing-Business-with-GoC**). It describes what you need to know before starting to prepare your bid, how to prepare a proposal, how proposals are evaluated, how the winning proposal will be selected, and how suppliers should follow up after the evaluation process. The Contracts Canada Web site is also helpful (**tinyurl.com/writing-tips-for-proposals**). Staff with the Office of Small and Medium Enterprises can provide you with general advice, too (but they can't help you with a specific proposal that you're writing). For contact information, see Chapter 5, "Getting Started."

For more insight from a private sector viewpoint, check out *Ottawa Business Journal* columnist Keith Parker's column on preparing proposals for the Government of Canada (search for "Keith Parker" at **www.obj. ca**. For columns prior to 2010, you'll need to click on "OBJ Archives 1999-2009" in the right-hand navigation).

Finally, if you just can't bear to tackle writing a proposal on your own, hire a writer from a proposal development company. To find candidates, Google "proposal development" (or "proposal management") companies for your city or region.

Chapter 7

Marketing Yourself

The importance of having an Internet presence

Everybody needs a Web site. A business doesn't look bona fide without one. You wouldn't think it necessary in this day and age to have to state that, but a glance through the Documents Request List on **www. merx.com** still reveals companies—usually individuals—who have no Web site.

For sole proprietors offering professional services, a Web site needn't be more than about five pages. It's simply a place to park your portfolio, detail recent projects you've spearheaded, show samples of your work by linking to client Web sites, share client testimonials and provide contact information so that people can reach you to get quotes on jobs.

On your Web site—and in any other marketing material—you should list your standing offer / supply arrangement award numbers, provided a department/agency has not imposed restrictions on advertising this information. Rumour has it that the federal government's Standing Offer Index is not a great search engine. Listing your award numbers makes life easier for federal employers who want to secure your services.

Getting a Web site designed doesn't need to be expensive, and the design firm you hire can teach you how to update your own Web site. Make sure that your site is registered with Google and other search engines so that people can find you online.

And whether you have a Web site or not, you should be on **www. linkedin.com**, the social networking site for professionals. There are currently more than 1,000 Government of Canada employees on LinkedIn. This is a chance to make direct contact with some of them through your other connections and let your unique talents be known to this audience. As well, LinkedIn profiles rank near the top of search engine results, a bonus when potential government clients are trying to learn more about you.

If you're already on LinkedIn, you also know that headhunters actively use this medium these days to try to recruit qualified professionals. Some have started their own groups on generic topics in order to reel in potential candidates.

The importance of having an Internet presence became sadly obvious to me when I met the project authority for one of my standing offers. A project authority is your first point of contact in a department. He or she is the one who lines up standing offer holders with eligible contracts in their department.

In this case, this was the first time the project authority and I had met face-to-face, and we had a chance to chat for a while. His department was one of those that PWGSC shops for, so while PWGSC and certain officials from his department had evaluated my bid, he personally had never seen it.

Tip

The fiscal year begins in April. Once budgets/plans are set, the Canadian government does a lot of spending between October and December.

All he had was a copy of a typical 19-page PWGSC standing offer award, and the only information it contained about me was my name, phone number, fax number, e-mail address and the rates I had quoted in my financial offer. That's all. It didn't even include my Web site address.

I had just assumed that the project authority would have seen my very detailed technical offer, the one that I had sweated blood over for more than a week, the one with the painstaking descriptions of every single editing project I had worked on for the past 24 months. He hadn't. He knew absolutely nothing about me.

So he told me he Googled me. That's how he found out I had experience with plain language writing and editing. It was on my Web site. And he was looking for someone who could do plain language editing.

The moral of this story is that if you don't have a Web site, you may not know how many opportunities you're missing out on.

Do your research first

When the time comes to get out there and sell yourself, don't mow down everyone in sight with your queries. Instead, target federal departments, agencies and Crown corporations that are a good match for your skills and experience. Learn as much as you can about them before making contact. The less time they have to spend getting you up to speed on critical issues of the day, the more attractive—and competent—a contractor you appear to them. Here are some ways to find out what initiatives they're working on:

- Check a department's Web site for its latest annual *Report on Plans and Priorities* and *Departmental Performance Report.*

- Scrutinize House of Commons and Senate Committee reports on a wide array of topics, plus government responses to committees that reveal how the Government of Canada is responding to current issues (go to **tinyurl.com/HoC-committees** and **tinyurl.com/Senate-committees**).

- Put a Google Alert on a government topic to get e-mail updates on media coverage.

- Read up on Treasury Board of Canada Secretariat federal policies that may affect your field; for example, *Policy on Management of Information Technology* if you work in high tech, or *Communications Policy of the Government of Canada* if you are a communications specialist (go to **www.tbs-sct. gc.ca** and click on "Policies" in the left-hand navigation). The Treasury Board of Canada Secretariat is responsible for the general management of Canadian government initiatives, issues and activities across all policy sectors.

- Follow a federal department or agency on Twitter and Linkedin.com to get updates on new initiatives, press releases, jobs, who is being hired and promoted, and more. (Note: not all Government of Canada departments / agencies use social media yet.)

- Get business and political insights on federal government issues courtesy of the *Ottawa Business Journal* (**www.obj.ca**), the Cable Public Affairs Channel, or CPAC (**www.cpac.ca**), and *The Hill Times* (www.thehilltimes.ca). A subscription for back issues of *The Hill Times* is required.

Speaking of doing your research . . . understand that the government fiscal year runs from April to March. As a rule, budgets are established between April and June, programs and work plans are set up between July and September, and purchasing is done between October and December. (And as seasoned government contractors know, fanatical amounts of work are done between January and March as departments approach fiscal year-end and are forced to use up the dollars in their budget.)

This doesn't mean that you'll only get contracts between October and December. I've had contracts come through at all times of the year. But it's good to be especially primed for business in the fall. Temp agencies and others are very active at that time. In 2009, during the week before Christmas, I was one of five companies invited by a government agency to bid on a three-month Web writing project scheduled to run immediately after the holidays, from January to March. Talk about last-minute Christmas shopping!

Cold-call key government contacts

Selling yourself is awkward—I know. But face it. You're going to be a small fish in a big pool of suppliers, all looking to cash in on the federal government marketplace. You need to distinguish yourself from the crowd and elaborate on your areas of expertise. Believe me, you'll be doing federal buyers a favour by letting them know about your skills and availability. Government employees are often in a time crunch to get projects done. The last contractor they spoke with may be the first one they'll call with an opportunity.

PWGSC constantly reminds suppliers that registering in databases is only the first step. Once you've registered in supplier databases, you need to contact PWGSC procurement officers, as well as departmental materiel managers and managers related to your field of work. (Remember to e-mail managers in your field of work rather than phone them.) Refer back to Chapter 4, "Where to Look for Contracts," for contact information for all of these key players.

You may find the selling process less awkward if you give materiel managers a quick phone call to introduce yourself first. Explain what you do, then tell them that you'll be sending a more detailed e-mail that includes your résumé. That way, the materiel manager doesn't have to commit to anything right off the bat, and can mull over your résumé while considering current departmental needs. It would also be handy to send along a .pdf of a brochure or information kit about your company. It doesn't have to be complex. I pulled together an information kit with graphics of a few Web sites I'd written or edited, and reports, newsletters and PowerPoint presentations I'd done. That, with some client testimonials, can spruce up your company profile.

For more suggestions on promoting yourself to the federal government, go to Contracts Canada's Web site at **tinyurl.com/ promoting-goods-services**. You should also check out "Step 3: Promoting Yourself" in the Office of Small and Medium Enterprises' *Your Guide to Doing Business with the Government of Canada* (**tinyurl. com/Doing-Business-with-GoC**).

Market yourself even after you've been awarded a standing offer

A common complaint that I've heard from colleagues is that sometimes, even after being awarded a standing offer, they don't get any work. Here again, it's a case of having to market yourself so that you stand out from the competition.

E-mail your project authority or contract authority on a regular basis to let them know you're available. Tell them when you're free over the summer months. Perhaps you can help them out while regular staff are on holidays. Send them a Christmas card to extend your best wishes, and remind them again that you're available to help out during holidays, if this is your situation.

Another good idea is to ask if the two of you could meet for a coffee to discuss your particular talents and how you could help out the department. I've done that several times now. In fact, it was the suggestion of one of my project authorities that we meet for lunch or coffee. We ended up going out for coffee, but what I thought would be a short 20-minute get-together turned into an hour-and-a-half-long meeting where we talked about his department, the challenges it faced, his desire to incorporate plain language into as many communication materials as possible, and so on.

As our meeting was winding down, I told him that a common dilemma my fellow editors faced was that of not getting any work despite being awarded a standing offer. I asked him if, from his experience, he felt it would be kosher for potential suppliers to call up a project authority for coffee or lunch, just as we were doing, to talk shop.

He said absolutely (this was when he told me he only learned about my background by Googling me). It helps to cement a relationship, and it's human nature to feel somewhat closer to someone once you've met them. People will be more likely to trust you, and think of you in a pinch, assuming you provide top-notch service.

And if you do receive a call-up for work, always offer to meet with that client at any point during the project to answer questions in person, if that would be helpful to him or her. Clients appreciate the offer. Not only does a face-to-face meeting help create rapport, it may expedite the work process as well.

A final note to help foster good business relations with federal government clients. Public servants are bound by the *Values and Ethics Code for the Public Service* (**tinyurl.com/values-ethics**), and both public servants and suppliers must abide by the *Code of Conduct for Procurement* (**tinyurl.com/procurement-code**). Suppliers should especially familiarize themselves with this last document, which spells out mutual expectations among all involved in the procurement process. Suppliers should also be aware of restrictions laid out in the *Values and Ethics Code for the Public Service*. Civil servants are not allowed to accept gifts such as "free or discounted admission to sporting and cultural events arising out of an actual or potential business relationship directly related to the public servant's official duties." And while they are permitted to accept items of minimal value such as simple meals, I can attest that in two instances when I met government acquaintances for coffee, they would not allow me to buy them a cup of coffee. Coming from a private-sector background, it felt rude not to buy my client a coffee. But rather than put your client in an awkward situation, just accept that you'll both be going Dutch.

> **Tip**
>
> Be accessible. Check your e-mail and cell phone regularly. Senior civil servants carry BlackBerrys and will respond to you at night on work.

Subcontract with other companies

The Office of Small and Medium Enterprises strongly urges companies to pursue subcontracting when looking to work with the Government of Canada. This makes sense, as it leads to greater efficiencies all around. As when dealing with temp agencies, subcontracting with companies that have already been awarded contracts is a good way to gain work experience with the Canadian government, if you lack this. There are several ways to sleuth out subcontracting opportunities:

- Search the Contract History database in Contracts Canada's Web site (**tinyurl.com/Contract-History**). It provides information on contracts awarded by PWGSC over the past three years, including the name of the vendor, its general address, the approximate number of employees and the business sector it's in, the number and dollar value of the contract, the procurement method used for awarding the contract, the purchasing department (that's PWGSC), and the client department, its address, and contact information. Contract History is a great tool. Practice using it for best results. The "Help" section provides search examples to test out, so that you get the hang of it.

- The Treasury Board of Canada Secretariat (**tinyurl.com/TBS-contracts-awarded**) lists all contracts over $10,000 awarded, broken down by fiscal quarter. These are static reports, not a searchable database. You can narrow your search by checking out the "Proactive Disclosure" section of each department's Web site for contract awards (look for the link in the bottom left-hand corner of the home page).

- MERX (**www.merx.com**) lists contracts awarded for departments that make such information available. Among other tidbits, it provides the name and address of the vendor as well as the name and address of the buyer, the contract number, date awarded, and dollar value of the award. Click on "Awards" in the drop-down box headed by "Open Opportunities," and enter a search term in the field to the left.

- A non-profit watchdog group called VisibleGovernment. ca runs **disclosed.ca**, a searchable database with info on contract awards culled from more than 100 federal government Web sites. Warning: contract award dates appear to be recent only to 2008, although the contract period in some cases spans several years.

Take advantage of other federal programs

- Get listed for free in Industry Canada's Canadian Company Capabilities directory (**tinyurl.com/cdn-company-capabilities**), a searchable database of 60,000-plus Canadian companies and their products and services. More than half a million domestic and international companies browse the database every month looking for Canadian businesses.

- If your business is Aboriginal-owned, register in the Aboriginal Business Directory (**tinyurl.com/Aboriginal-Biz-Directory**) to ensure you don't miss out on federal government opportunities available to you under the Procurement Strategy for Aboriginal Business.

- Thoroughly explore the Canada Business site (**www.canadabusiness.ca**). It sets the gold standard in government business Web sites with tons of up-to-the-minute articles on every aspect of running a small or medium-sized business in Canada. Canada Business has service centres across Canada. Follow Canada Business on Twitter, too, for great business tips.

- Several federal agencies provide financial aid, export assistance and more. The Business Development Bank of Canada (**www.bdc.ca**) delivers financial, investment and consulting services to Canadian small businesses, with a special focus on the technology and export sectors. Export Development Canada (**www.edc.ca**) offers insurance, guarantees and long-term loans to help exporters and investors compete in international markets.

Some final tips

- Find out if the Canadian General Standards Board (**tinyurl. com/Cdn-General-Standards-Board**) or other standards agencies have developed standards for your services. If so, get your services up to par and get listed on the Board's program list for your commodity. The government uses program lists to find pre-qualified suppliers.

- If your services qualify as being "green," register them with a government-sponsored directory of green products. For more information, visit:
  ◊ Office of Greening Government Operations (**www.tpsgc-pwgsc.gc.ca/ecologisation-greening**)
  ◊ Office of Energy Efficiency (**oee.nrcan.gc.ca**)
  ◊ EcoLogo Program (**www.ecologo.org**)

- Do an excellent job (but you already do that, don't you!) and be fast. Quick, reliable turnaround is valued tremendously by the feds, and it's an area where small, nimble companies can excel.

- Have a complaint about a contract? Contact the new Office of the Procurement Ombudsman (**opo-boa.gc.ca**) for service contracts below $100,000, or the administration of a contract regardless of its dollar value. For contracts covered by trade agreements, get in touch with the Canadian International Trade Tribunal (**www.citt.gc.ca**).

Chapter 8

Getting Government Security Clearance

No clearance? No sweat

Some contracts and government tenders require that you and your employees be cleared or screened for security or reliability. If you don't have the appropriate level of clearance when bidding on a job, ask in your bid that the buyer sponsor you. Temp agencies, too, can sponsor you in an attempt to get government security clearance. According to PWGSC's Industrial Security Directorate, a required security level may be obtained after a contractor has been selected, provided the bid solicitation does not contain "Protected"/"Classified" information elements.

Obtaining reliability status, the lowest level of clearance, is fairly straightforward and may be done in a matter of days.

However, you will need an industrial facility security clearance if you want to bid on contracts requiring access to sensitive or classified material, information or government buildings.

In the case of secret clearance, it can take up to a year before your approval comes through. And don't assume the process has automatically begun once you've been awarded a standing offer. Keep in touch with the buyer to ensure things are underway. Expect to be asked to fill out a number of complex forms detailing your personal and work history.

Learn more about federal government security clearance at **tinyurl. com/security-clearance**. You can also call 1-866-368-4646 (in the National Capital Region, it's 613-948-4176) or e-mail ncr.ciisd@tpsgc-pwgsc.gc.ca.

The value of a secret clearance

Once your secret clearance comes through, it opens up many more doors for you. Since there are far fewer secret-cleared personnel, temp agencies may notify you more often about opportunities.

A few tips to remember:

- Don't let your secret clearance lapse. Six months before it's set to expire, contact PWGSC again to get the process started for renewing your clearance. A secret clearance lasts 10 years (the same goes for enhanced clearance).

- Don't advertise that you have secret facility security clearance on your Web site or in any other public medium. The Industrial Security Directorate of PWGSC warns you against doing this. They say it's for your own good. You could become the target of a break-in if people thought you had valuable secret documents on your premises.

Tip

If you don't meet a tender's security requirements (and "Protected"/"Classified" information isn't a factor), ask in your bid that the buyer sponsor you.

Chapter 9

Getting Work with Other Governments

Tapping into other public sector markets in Canada and globally

Once you've mastered the learning curve for the federal government's procurement process, you may find yourself getting that tingly "if I can make it there, I can make it anywhere!" feeling. In fact, you might consider expanding into other government markets. After all, government procurement processes share some common features. What's more, governments often accept experience gained working with other types of governments in bid submissions.

- Before taking the plunge, read the very helpful "Selling to Governments" section on the Canada Business Web site (**www.canadabusiness.ca**). It enumerates the pros and cons of such an undertaking, and provides info and links to sites dedicated to explaining how to do business with Canadian provincial, territorial and municipal governments, as well as with foreign governments.

- MARCAN (**www.marcan.net**) is a Canadian public sector procurement portal that provides Web links to all provincial and territorial procurement agencies, explains in which newspapers the provincial or territorial governments advertise their government tenders, and gives contact information for suppliers who want to get on source lists.

- Another major e-tendering portal for certain Canadian public and private sector entities is Biddingo (**www. biddingo.com**). There is a subscription fee, but a bonus is that subscribers automatically get to register in Biddingo's database of suppliers, used by purchasing managers.

- The Canadian Commercial Corporation (**www.ccc. ca**) specializes in government contracts in aerospace and defence (clients include the U.S. Department of Defense and NASA), and in countries experiencing rapid growth and industrialization. The Canadian Commercial Corporation helps Canadian companies export goods and services by identifying Canadian firms to foreign governments and international agencies.

- If you're a housing expert, apply to join the Canada Mortgage and Housing Corporation (CMHC) International Professional Pool (**tinyurl.com/CMHC-pool**) so that you can be considered for work with the CMHC when international projects come up in your field of expertise.

- Pitch your talents to the largest economy in the world: the United States. Canada is a partner to international agreements that eliminate trade barriers for Canadian businesses, such as NAFTA and the World Trade Organization Agreement on Government Procurement. Another plus: the U.S. fiscal year runs from October 1 to September 30 and like Canada, the U.S. government does lots of fourth-quarter spending. That means there is big money to be made in July through September, which nicely bookends the Canadian government's January-to-March fiscal year-end spending rush. To learn more, explore the Canadian government Web site, **sell2usgov.ca**. It's a one-stop shop for doing business with the U.S. federal government. Be aware that under NAFTA and/or the World Trade Organization Agreement on Government Procurement, some commodities are excluded, along with the following services:
  ◊ research and development
  ◊ health and social services
  ◊ financial and related services
  ◊ utilities, and
  ◊ communications, photographic, mapping, printing and
    publications services.

- Other agreements with a government procurement component are the Canada-Chile Free Trade Agreement, the Canada-Peru Free Trade Agreement, the Canada-Panama Free Trade Agreement, and Canada's trade negotiations with El Salvador, Guatemala, Honduras and Nicaragua (known as the "Central American Four"), CARICOM, Colombia, the Dominican Republic, Singapore and South Korea. Learn more about trade agreements at the Web sites of Foreign Affairs and International Trade Canada (**tinyurl.com/Foreign-Affairs-trade**) and Contracts Canada (**tinyurl.com/trade-agreements**). The Foreign Affairs site also details the February 2010 Canada-U.S. Agreement on Government Procurement, which allows Canadian companies to participate in U.S. infrastructure projects financed under the *American Recovery and Reinvestment Act*. Elsewhere on the Foreign Affairs site, you can read about another massive trade agreement under negotiation, the proposed Canada-European Union Comprehensive Economic and Trade Agreement (**tinyurl.com/Canada-EU-trade**).

Tip

The U.S. government's fiscal year starts in October, and the U.S. does lots of spending in the fourth quarter ending in September.

Chapter 10

Important Web Links

Contracts Canada
www.contractscanada.gc.ca

Office of Small and Medium Enterprises
www.tpsgc-pwgsc.gc.ca/app-acq/pme-sme/index-eng.html
(Or, tinyurl.com/Office-of-SME.)

Public Works and Government Services Canada (click on "Buying and Selling")
www.tpsgc-pwgsc.gc.ca

Supplier Registration Information services
www.contractscanada.gc.ca/inscr-rgstr-eng.html
(Or, tinyurl.com/Supplier-Registration.)

Professional Services Online
www.tpsgc-pwgsc.gc.ca/app-acq/sp-ps/index-eng.html
(Or, tinyurl.com/PS-Online.)

SELECT
https://select.pwgsc-tpsgc.gc.ca/index-eng.cfm?af=ZnVzZWFjdGlvbj1sb2d
pbi5mYV9kc3BfaW50cm8=&lang=eng (Or, tinyurl.com/SELECT-SA.)

MERX
www.merx.com

Government Electronic Directory Services
sage-geds.tpsgc-pwgsc.gc.ca

Departmental Materiel Managers
www.contractscanada.gc.ca/gmm-dmm-eng.html
(Or, tinyurl.com/materiel-managers.)

Procurement Allocation Directory

pad.contractscanada.gc.ca/index-eng.cfm?af=ZnVzZWFjdGlvbj1pbmZ
vLmludHJvJmlkPTI=&lang=eng
(Or, tinyurl.com/PAD-Gov-Canada.)

Industrial Security Directorate, Public Works and Government Services Canada

www.ssi-iss.tpsgc-pwgsc.gc.ca/index-eng.html
(Or, tinyurl.com/security-clearance.)

Canada Business—Services for Entrepreneurs

www.canadabusiness.ca

"How to Do Business with the Government of Canada," TD Canada Trust archived Webinar

www.tdcanadatrust.com/smallbusiness/government_procurement.jsp
(Or, tinyurl.com/TD-Canada-Trust-Webinar.)

Office of the Procurement Ombudsman

opo-boa.gc.ca

Ottawa Business Journal

- *Ottawa Business Journal* contributor Keith Parker's column on preparing federal government proposals (search for "Keith Parker" at www.obj.ca. For columns prior to 2010, click on "OBJ Archives 1999-2009" in the right-hand navigation.)

- *Ottawa Business Journal* Procurement blog
procurementblog.obj.ca

Summit Magazine: Canada's magazine on public sector purchasing

www.summitconnects.com

Tip

For great business leads, follow Canada Business on Twitter, too (twitter.com/CanadaBusiness).

Appendix A

Firms under the Temporary Help Services On-Line System (National Capital Region)

1019837 Ontario Inc.
(Dynamic Personnel Consultants)
Suite 404
222 Somerset St. W.
Ottawa ON K2P 2G3
Phone: (613) 567-8886
Fax: (613) 567-8822
E-mail: hr@dynamicpersonnel.com
Web site: www.dynamicpersonnel.com

1092009 Ontario Inc.
(Personnel Force)
Suite 701
350 Sparks St.
Ottawa ON K1R 7S8
Phone: (613) 237-9798
Fax: (613) 237-7752
E-mail: info@personnelforce.com
Web site: www.personnelforce.com

175213 Canada Inc.
(Samson & Associates)
85 Victoria St.
Gatineau QC J8X 2A3
Phone: (819) 772-0044
Fax: (819) 595-9094
E-mail: samson@samson.ca
Web site: samson.ca

2093030 Ontario Inc.
(Turtle Island Staffing)
Suite 701
222 Somerset St. W.
Ottawa ON K2P 2G3
Phone: (613) 567-8828
Fax: (613) 567-4898
E-mail: hr@turtleislandstaffing.com
Web site: www.turtleislandstaffing.com

3056058 Canada Inc.
(C.L.A. Personnel)
424-C Queen St.
Ottawa ON K1R 5A8
Phone: (613) 567-0045
Fax: (613) 567-0049
E-mail: (online form)
Web site: www.clapersonnel.ca

3178935 Canada Inc.
(Hunt Personnel/Temporarily Yours)
Suite 300
220 Laurier Ave. W.
Ottawa ON K1P 5Z9
Phone: (613) 238-8801
Fax: (613) 238-5586
E-mail: ottawa@hunt.ca
Web site: www.hunt.ca

3852946 Canada Inc.
(Maxsys Aboriginal Services)
Suite B
173 Dalhousie St.
Ottawa ON K1N 7C7
Phone: (613) 562-9943
Toll-free phone: 1-800-429-5177
Fax: (613) 241-6742
Toll-free fax: 1-866-565-0006
E-mail: hr@maxsys.ca
Web site: www.maxsys.ca

529040 Ontario Inc. and 880382
Ontario Inc.
(GSI International Consulting)
Suite 300
70 University Ave.
Toronto ON M5J 2M4
Phone: (416) 777-2525
Fax: (416) 777-2547
E-mail: smcdonnell@gsigroup.com
Web site: prdwww.gsigroup.com

802732 Ontario Inc.
(The Associates Group of
Companies)
Suite 700
222 Somerset St. W.
Ottawa ON K2P 2G3
Phone: (613) 567-0222
Fax: (613) 567-6441
E-mail (for professional contracts):
resumes@taghr.com
Web site: www.taghr.com

A S G Inc.
Suite 8
1010 Polytek Dr.
Ottawa ON K1J 9H8
Phone: (613) 749-8353
Fax: (613) 749-2908
E-mail: cmayville@asg-ottawa.com
Web site: www.asg-ottawa.com

A. Net Solutions Inc.
196A Papineau St.
Gatineau QC J8X 1W2
Phone: (819) 777-9174
Toll-free phone: 1-877-777-9174
Fax: (819) 777-4091
Toll-free fax: 1-877-777-4091
E-mail: anoronha@anetsolutions.com
Web site: anetsolutions.ca

Access Corporate Technologies, Inc.
Suite 620
1600 Carling Ave.
Ottawa ON K1Z 1G3
Phone: (613) 236-6114
Fax: (613) 236-5552
E-mail: careers@accesscorp.ca
Web site: www.accesscorp.ca

Action Personnel of Ottawa-Hull Ltd.
Suite 200
280 Albert St.
Ottawa ON K1P 5G8
Phone: (613) 238-8511
Fax: (613) 230-8380
E-mail: info@actionpersonnel.ca
Web site: www.actionpersonnel.ca

Adecco Employment Services
Limited
Suite 308
126 York St.
Ottawa ON K1N 5T5
Phone: (613) 244-0241
Toll-free phone: 1-866-565-0559
E-mail: (online form)
Web site: www.adecco.ca/ottawa-jobs.htm

ADGA Group Consultants Inc. Suite 600 116 Albert St. Ottawa ON K1P 5G3 Phone: (613) 237-3022 E-mail: adga@adga.ca Web site: www.adga.ca	**ADRM Technology Consulting Group Corp.** 45 St. Andrew St. Ottawa ON K1N 5E8 Phone: (613) 241-8080 Fax: (613) 241-7324 E-mail: paul.petrie@adrmtec.com Web site: www.adrmtec.com
Advantage Personnel Ltd. Suite 307 124 O'Connor St. Ottawa ON K1P 5M9 Phone: (613) 232-0100 Fax: (613) 232-6637 Toll-free fax: 1-800-923-8077 E-mail: ottawa@onyourteam.com Web site: www.onyourteam.com	**AIM—Adirondack Information Management Inc.** Suite 126 130 Albert St. Ottawa ON K1P 5G4 Phone: (613) 230-6991 E-mail: info@adirondackhr.ca Web site: adirondackim.ca
Ajilon Canada Inc. Suite 1206 155 Queen St. Ottawa ON K1P 6L1 Phone: (613) 786-3106 Toll-free phone: (888) 817-4632 Fax: (613) 567-3341 E-mail: ottawa@ajilon.com Web site: www.ajilon.ca	**Alcea Technologies Inc.** 424 Parkdale Ave. Ottawa ON K1Y 1H1 Phone: (613) 563-9595 Toll-free phone: 1-877-321-4463 Fax: (613) 563-9494 E-mail: info@alceatech.com Web site: www.alceatech.com
Alliance Personnel Inc. Suite 1201 130 Albert St. Ottawa ON K1P 5G4 Phone: (613) 235-9191 Fax: (613) 235-6464 E-mail: info@apihr.ca Web site: www.apihr.ca	**Altis Human Resources (Ottawa) Inc.** Suite 302 102 Bank St. Ottawa ON K1P 5N4 Phone: (613) 230-5350 Fax: (613) 230-1623 E-mail: altisSPR@altisSPR.com Web site: www.altishr.com

AMITA Corporation
Suite 500
1420 Blair Place
Gloucester ON K1J 9L8
Phone: (613) 742-6482
Toll-free phone: 1-800-566-8883
Fax: (613) 742-8188
E-mail: jobs@amita.com
Web site: www.amita.com

AMTEK Engineering Services Ltd.
1676 Bank St.
Ottawa ON K1V 7Y6
Phone: (613) 749-3990
Fax: (613) 749-5167
E-mail: (Choose the e-mail for your career type here: www.amtekcdn.com/employment/gen_sub.asp)
Web site: www.amtekcdn.com

APS—Antian Professional Services Inc.
1122 Wellington St. W.
Ottawa ON K1Y 2Y7
Phone: (613) 233-6464
Fax: (613) 233-5995
Toll-free fax: 1-888-758-1122
E-mail: rm.sherwood@antian.ca
Web site: www.antian.ca

Artemp Personnel Services Inc.
Suite 104
294 Albert St.
Ottawa ON K1P 6E6
Phone: (613) 232-9767
Fax: (613) 232-7050
E-mail: info@artemp.ca
Web site: www.artemp.ca

Azur Human Resources Ltd.
Suite 1002
275 Slater St.
Ottawa ON K1P 5H9
Phone: (613) 238-4008
Fax: (613) 288-2145
E-mail: azurhr@azurhr.com
Web site: www.azurhr.com

B D M K Consultants Inc.
Suite 701
280 Albert St.
Ottawa ON K1P 5G8
Phone: (613) 233-4343
Fax: (613) 233-0494
E-mail: carissa.buckley@bdmk.ca
Web site: None

BBG Management
Suite 111
1750 Courtwood Cres.
Ottawa ON K2C 2B5
Phone: (613) 482-4437
Fax: (613) 216-9762
E-mail: jobs@bbgmanagement.com
Web site: www.bbgmanagement.com

BiR Consulting Inc.
37 San Remo Private
Ottawa ON K1G 5X9
Phone: (819) 459-3284
Fax: (819) 459-2957
E-mail: irene@birconsulting.ca or blair@birconsulting.ca
Web site: www.birconsulting.ca

BMCI Consulting Inc. Suite 1203 60 Queen St. Ottawa ON K1P 5Y7 Phone: (613) 738-7514 Fax: (613) 733-7451 E-mail: bmci@travel-net.com Web site: www.bmcicompanies.com	**Brainhunter (Ottawa) Inc.** Suite 600 1545 Carling Ave. Ottawa ON K1Z 8P9 Phone: (613) 789-7000 Fax: (613) 722-8756 Toll-free: 1-877-761-9436 E-mail: support@brainhunter.com
Brican Personnel Inc. **(SPI Consultants)** 1400 St Laurent Blvd. Ottawa ON K1K 4H4 Phone: (613) 590-1503 Fax: (613) 824-3593 E-mail: (online form) Web site: spi.ca	**Bronson Consulting Group** 6 Monkland Ave. Ottawa ON K1S 1Y9 Phone: (613) 787-2000 Fax: (613) 787-2011 E-mail: baird@bronson.ca Web site: www.bronson.ca
C I A—Conseillers en Informatique **d'affaires Inc.** Suite 405 200 Montcalm Blvd. Gatineau QC J8Y 3B5 Phone: (819) 771-6446 Fax: (819) 771-4101 E-mail: ottawa@cia.ca Web site: www.cia.ca	**Calian Ltd.** Suite 101 340 Legget Dr. Ottawa ON K2K 1Y6 Phone: (613) 599-8600 Fax: (613) 599-8650 Toll-free fax: 1-877-225-4264 E-mail: info@calian.com Web site: bts.calian.com
Canada Job One Inc. Suite 1100 One Nicholas St. Ottawa ON K1N 7B7 Phone: (613) 789-9911 Fax: (613) 789-7637 E-mail: ottawa@canadajobone.ca Web site: www.canadajobone.ca	**CGI Information Systems and** **Management Consultants Inc.** 14th floor 275 Slater St. Ottawa ON K1P 5H9 Phone: (613) 234-2155 Fax: (613) 234-6934 E-mail: web@cgi.com Web site: www.cgi.com

Confluence Consulting Inc. Suite 512 56 Sparks St. Ottawa ON K1P 5A9 Phone: (613) 235-2228 Fax: (613) 235-2229 E-mail: info@confluence.ca Web site: www.confluence.ca	**Conoscenti Technologies Inc.** Suite 320 384 Bank St. Ottawa ON K2P 1Y4 Phone: (613) 688-2200 Fax: (613) 688-2199 E-mail: sales@conoscenti.ca Web site: www.conoscenti.ca
Conseillers en Informatique d'affaires C I A Inc. Suite R-8 200 Montcalm St. Gatineau QC J8Y 3B5 Phone: (819) 771-6446 Fax: (819) 771-4101 E-mail: ottawa@cia.ca Web site: www.cia.ca	**Contract Community Inc.** 860 Berryside Rd. RR#1 Dunrobin ON K0A 1T0 Phone: (613) 832-5500 Fax: (613) 248-4721 E-mail: todd@contractcommunity.com Web site: contractcommunity.com
CORADIX Technology Consulting Ltd. Suite 1010 151 Slater St. Ottawa ON K1P 5H3 Phone: (613) 234-0800 Fax: (613) 234-0988 E-mail: hr@coradix.com Web site: www.coradix.com	**CSI Consulting Inc.** 109 York St. Ottawa ON K1N 5T4 Phone: (613) 291-8546 Fax: (613) 270-0230 E-mail: charles@csican.com Web site: www.csican.com
Dalian Enterprises and CORADIX Technology Consulting (in joint venture) Suite 1010 151 Slater St. Ottawa ON K1P 5H3 Phone: (613) 234-1995 Fax: (613) 234-0988 E-mail: hr@dalian.ca Web site: www.dalian.ca	**DAMA Consulting Services Limited** P.O. Box 211 Station B Ottawa ON K1P 6C4 Phone: (613) 748-0547 Fax: (613) 748-1908 Email: info@dama-consult.com Web site: www.dama-consult.com

DARE Human Resources Corporation Suite 900 275 Slater St. Ottawa ON K1P 5H9 Phone: (613) 238-3273 Fax: (613) 238-9532 E-mail: (online form) Web site: www.darehr.com	**David Aplin & Associates Inc.** Suite 910 350 Sparks St. Ottawa ON K1R 7S8 Phone: (613) 288-2211 Fax: (613) 288-0213 E-mail: Ottawa@aplin.com Web site: www.aplin.com
Design Group Staffing Inc. (The People Bank) Suite 100 130 Slater St. Ottawa ON K1P 6E2 Phone: (613) 234-8118 Fax: (613) 234-7365 Toll-free fax:1-888-234-8118 E-mail: ottawa@thepeoplebank.com Web site: www.thepeoplebank.com	**DLS Technology Corporation** Suite 501-502 1376 Bank St. Ottawa ON K1H 7Y3 Phone: (613) 249-8818 Fax: (613) 249-8816 Toll-free fax: 1-888-297-1225 E-mail: info@dlstech.com Web site: www.dlstech.com
Donna Cona Inc. Suite 100 106 Colonnade Rd. Ottawa ON K2E 7L6 Phone: (613) 234-5407 Fax: (613) 234-7761 E-mail: Contact@DonnaCona.com Web site: www.donnacona.com	**Drake International Inc.** Suite 1400 320 Bay St. Toronto ON M5H 4A6 Phone: (416) 216-1000 Fax: (416) 216-1109 E-mail: br-toronto.drake@hiredesk.net Web site: www.drakeintl.com/ca
e Networks Corporation Suite 520 1730 St Laurent Blvd. Ottawa ON K1G 5L1 Phone: (613) 526-4945 Fax: (613) 526-3641 E-mail: info@integranetworks.com Web site: www.integranetworks.com	**Eagle Professional Resources Inc.** Suite 902 170 Laurier Ave W. Ottawa ON K1P 5V5 Phone: (613) 234-1810 Toll-free phone: 1-888-798-8181 Fax: (613) 234-0797 Toll-free fax: 1-888-361-0579 E-mail: NESST@eagleonline.com Web site: www.eagleonline.com

Excel Human Resources Inc. (AltisSPR)	Equasion Business Technologies Consulting Inc.
Suite 300 102 Bank St. Ottawa ON K1P 5N4 Phone: (613) 230-5393 Fax: (613) 230-1623 E-mail: (online form) Web site: www1.excelhr.com	412 Piccadilly Ave. Ottawa ON K1Y 0H4 Phone: (613) 860-1629 Fax: (613) 860-1629 E-mail: info@equasion.ca Web site: www.equasion.ca
FMC Professionals Inc.	**Harrington Marketing Limited**
Suite 400 11 Rosemount Ave. Ottawa ON K1Y 4R8 Phone: (613) 728-9512 Fax: (613) 728-5298 E-mail: david.mann@fmcprofessionals.com Web site: www.fmcprofessionals.com	Suite 300 30 Metcalfe St. Ottawa ON K1P 5L4 Phone: (613) 236-4600 Fax: (613) 236-2192 E-mail: staffing@harringtonhr.com or it@harringtonhr.com Web site: www.harringtonhr.com
Hays Personnel Services (Canada) Inc.	**HDP Group Inc.**
Suite 1802 5775 Yonge St. North York ON M2M 4J1 Phone: (416) 223-4297 Fax: (416) 223-4232 E-mail: recruit@hays.ca Web site: www.hays.ca	Suite 807 151 Slater St. Ottawa ON K1P 5H3 Phone: (613) 567-5300 Fax: (613) 567-5563 E-mail: ottawa@hdpgroup.com Web site: www.hdpgroup.com
Helix Management Consulting Services Inc.	**Human Resource Capital Group Inc. (Spherion)**
Unit 7 1420 Youville Dr. Orleans ON K1C 7B3 Phone: (613) 830-3644 Fax: (613) 830-2983 E-mail: office@hmcs.on.ca Web site: www.hmcs.on.ca	Suite 120 440 Laurier Ave. W. Ottawa ON K1R 7X6 Phone: (613) 782-2333 Fax: (613) 782-2434 E-mail: ottawa@spherion.ca Web site: www.spherion.ca

Ian Martin Limited Suite 203 275 Slater St. Ottawa ON K1P 5H9 Phone: (613) 237-0155 Fax: (613) 237-2070 E-mail: oconnor@ianmartin.com Web site: www.ianmartin.com	**IBISKA Telecom Inc.** Suite 1810 130 Albert St. Ottawa ON K1P 5G4 Phone: (613) 234-4434 Fax: (613) 234-4356 E-mail: info@ibiska.com Web site: www.ibiska.com
IBM Canada Ltd. Suite 1610 340 Albert St. Ottawa ON K1R 7Y6 Phone: (613) 249-1202 Fax: (613) 249-8441 E-mail: (online form) Web site: www.ibm.com/ca	**InGenius Engineering Inc.** 350 Legget Dr. Kanata ON K2K 2W7 Phone: (613) 591-9002 E-mail: info@ingeniuspeople.com Web site: www.ingenius.com
Integra Networks Corporation Suite 520 1730 St Laurent Blvd. Ottawa ON K1G 5L1 Phone: (613) 526-4945 Fax: (613) 526-3641 E-mail: hr@integranetworks.com Web site: www.integranetworks.com	**IT Services Canada Inc.** Suite 100 1088 Somerset St. W. Ottawa ON K1Y 3C7 Phone: (613) 725-0463 Fax: (613) 725-3110 E-mail: info@itservicescanada.com Web site: www.itservicescanada.com
IT/Net Ottawa Inc. 116 Albert St. Ottawa ON K1P 5G3 Phone: (613) 234-8638 Fax: (613) 234-3323 E-mail: info@itnet.ca Web site: www.itnet.ca	**Kelly Sears Consulting Group Inc.** Suite 802 280 Albert St. Ottawa ON K1P 5G8 Phone: (613) 230-9943 Fax: (613) 234-3346 E-mail: info@kellysears.ca Web site: www.kellysears.ca

Kelly Services Centennial Towers 200 Kent St. Ottawa ON K2P 2J8 Phone: (613) 238-4801 Fax: (613) 230-8709 E-mail: 7630@kellyservices.com Web site: www.kellyservices.ca	**Labor Tek Personnel Services Ltd.** 1370 Triole St. Ottawa ON K1B 3M4 Phone: (613) 741-1128 Fax: (613) 741-1130 E-mail: jbeauchamp@labortek.com Web site: www.labortek.com
Lannick Contract Solutions Inc. Constitution Square III Suite 1200 340 Albert St. Ottawa ON K1R 7Y6 Phone: (613) 566-7048 Fax: (613) 566-7049 E-mail: csotelo@lannickcontract.com Web site: www.lannickcontract.com	**Lansdowne Technologies Inc.** Suite 1001 275 Slater St. Ottawa ON K1P 5H9 Phone: (613) 236-3333 Fax: (613) 236-4440 E-mail: info@lansdowne.com Web site: www.lansdowne.com
Leverage Technology Resources Inc. Suite 1 136 Lewis St. Ottawa ON K2P 0S7 Phone: (613) 238-5100 Fax: (613) 238-5100 E-mail: inquiries@leveragetek.ca Web site: www.leveragetek.ca	**LNW Consulting Inc.** 4th Floor 300 March Rd. Kanata ON K2K 2E2 Phone: (613) 592-8133 Fax: (613) 838-4107 E-mail: info@LNWConsulting Web site: www.lnwconsulting.com
Logic 2000 Inc. Suite 200 887 Richmond Rd. Ottawa ON K2A 0G8 Phone: (613) 728-1515 Fax: (613) 728-1552 E-mail: careers@logic2000.com Web site: www.logic2000.com	**Lumina IT Inc.** Suite 101 22 Antares Dr. Ottawa ON K2E 7Z6 Phone: (613) 482-6601 Fax: (613) 228-9787 E-mail: pvandijk@luminait.com Web site: www.luminait.com

Manpower Services Canada Limited Suite 123 171 Bank St. Ottawa ON K2P 1W5 Phone: (613) 237-1727 Toll-free fax: 1-877-837-3836 E-mail: Ottawa.ON-Professional@ na.manpower.com Web site: www.manpowerprofessional.com	**Marbek Resource Consultants Ltd.** Suite 300 222 Somerset St. W. Ottawa ON K2P 2G3 Phone: (613) 523-0784 Fax: (613) 523-0717 E-mail: info@marbek.ca Web site: www.marbek.ca
Maxsys Professionals & Solutions Incorporated Suite A 173 Dalhousie St. Ottawa ON K1N 7C7 Phone: (613) 562-9943 Toll-free phone: 1-800-429-5177 Fax: (613) 241-6742 Toll-free fax: 1-866-565-0006 E-mail: hr@maxsys.ca Web site: www.maxsys.ca	**MCO Business Group Inc.** Suite 400 11 Rosemount Ave. Ottawa ON K1Y 4R8 Phone: (613) 728-2188 Toll-free phone: 1-866-861-9525 Fax: (613) 728-5298 E-mail: mco@mco.ca Web site: www.mco.ca
Mindwire Inc. Suite 200 950 Gladstone Ave. Ottawa ON K1Y 3E6 Phone: (613) 729-8800 Toll-free fax: 1-866-589-7240 E-mail: info@mindwire.ca Web site: www.mindwire.ca	**MSC Maplesoft Consulting Inc.** Suite 100 408 Churchill Ave. Ottawa ON K1Z 5C6 Phone: (613) 226-9993 Toll-free phone: 1-866-MAPLE02 Fax: (613) 226-8986 E-mail: info@maplesoftconsulting.com Web site: wwwmaplesoftconsulting.com
Navatar Ltd. Suite 300 85 Albert St. Ottawa ON K1P 6A4 Phone: (613) 594-9554 Fax: (613) 288-0499 E-mail: info@navatar.ca Web site: None	**New Technologies Inc.** Suite 406 300 March Rd. Kanata ON K2K 2E2 Phone: (613) 592-4009 E-mail: None Web site: None

Night Hawk Technologies Inc. Unit 380 400 Alexandre Taché Blvd. Gatineau QC J9A 1M5 Phone: (819) 771-5054 Fax: (819) 771-8384 E-mail: careers@marcomm.ca Web site: www.marcomm.ca	**NIVA Inc., Stiff Sentences** **Incorporated (in joint venture)** Suite 200 30 Murray St. Ottawa ON K1N 5M4 Phone: (613) 737-6000 E-mail: info@niva.com Web site: www.niva.com
Northern Brainwaves Consulting **Group Inc.** **(MSC Maplesoft Consulting Inc.)** 352 Danforth Ave. Ottawa ON K2A 0E2 Phone: (613) 226-9993 E-mail: info@maplesoftconsulting.com Web site: www.maplesoftconsulting.com	**Paul Pollack Personnel Ltd.** Suite 702 225 Metcalfe St. Ottawa ON K2P 1P9 Phone: (613) 238-2233 Fax: (613) 238-4407 E-mail: pollack.group@pollackgroup.com Web site: www.pollackgroup.com
Personnel Outaouais Inc. Suite 200 A 92 St-Raymond Blvd. Gatineau QC J8Y 1S7 Phone: (819) 778-7020 Toll-free phone: 1-888-778-7020 Fax: (819) 778-6534 E-mail: emploi@personneloutaouais.com Web site: www.personneloutaouais.com	**Pleiad Canada Inc.** 560 Churchill Ave. N. Ottawa ON K1Z 5E5 Phone: (613) 722-9902 Fax: (613) 728-4542 E-mail: corporate@pleiad.ca Web site: www.pleiad.ca
Portage Personnel Inc. 201-5 Laval Gatineau QC J8X 3G6 Phone: (819) 770-6918 Fax: (819) 777-8367 E-mail: info@portagepersonnel.ca Web site: www.temphelp.ca	**Pricewaterhouse Coopers LLP** Suite 800 99 Bank St. Ottawa ON K1P 1E4 Phone: (613) 237-3702 E-mail: (online form) Web site: www.pwc.com

PROEX Inc. Unit B 273 St. Patrick St. Ottawa ON K1N 5K4 Phone: (613) 244-0871 Toll-free phone: 1-877-717-7639 E-mail: Ottawa@proex.ca Web site: www.proex.ca	**Professional Computer Consultants Group Ltd.** Suite 600 300 March Rd. Kanata ON K2K 2E2 Tel: (613) 270-9339 Fax: (613) 270-9449 E-mail: ottawa@procom.ca Web site: www.procom.ca
Prolity Corporation 715 Canary St. Ottawa ON K4B 1H3 Phone: (613) 232-2869 Fax: (613) 232-5305 E-mail: (online form) Web site: www.prolity.com	**Prologic Systems Ltd.** Suite 206 75 Albert St. Ottawa ON K1P 5E7 Phone: (613) 238-1376 Fax: (613) 238-2347 E-mail: liz@prologicsystems.ca Web site: www.prologicsystems.ca
Promaxis Systems Inc. 2385 St. Laurent Blvd. Ottawa ON K1G 6C3 Phone: (613) 737-2112 Fax: (613) 737-0229 E-mail: info@promaxis.com Web site: www.promaxis.com	**Public History Inc.** Suite 200 377 Dalhousie St. Ottawa ON K1N 9N8 Phone: (613) 236-0713 Fax: (613) 236-3961 E-mail: ottawa@publichistory.ca Web site: www.publichistory.ca
QMR Staffing Solutions Incorporated Suite 906 75 Albert St. Ottawa ON K1P 5E7 Phone: (613) 234-4972 Fax: (613) 234-6654 Toll-free fax: 1-800-592-5103 E-mail: info@qmrstaffing.com Web site: www.qmrstaffing.com	**Quantum Management Services Ltd.** Suite 500 275 Slater Ave. Ottawa ON K1P 5H9 Phone: (613) 237-8888 Fax: (613) 230-7711 E-mail: webmaster@quantum.ca Web site: www.quantum.ca

Randstad Interim Inc. 52 Elgin St. Ottawa ON K1P 5K6 Phone: (613) 688-5560 Fax: (613) 688-5566 E-mail: (online form) Web site: www.randstad.ca	**Robert Half Canada Inc.** Suite 520 360 Albert St. Ottawa ON K1R 7X7 Phone: (613) 236-4253 Fax: (613) 236-8301 E-mail: Ottawa@accountemps.com Web site: www.roberthalf.ca
Robertson & Company Ltd. Suite 1104 1200 Bay St. Toronto ON M5R 2A5 Phone: (416) 929-0226 Fax: (416) 929-5549 E-mail: reception@ robertsonandcompany.net Web site: www.robertsonandcompany.net	**S I Systems Ltd.** Suite 1200 130 Slater St. Ottawa ON K1P 6E2 Phone: (613) 786-3290 Fax: (613) 786-3291 E-mail: (online form) Web site: www.sisystems.com
SOMOS Consulting Group Ltd. Suite 100 4019 Carling Ave. Ottawa ON K2K 2A3 Phone: (613) 592-5050 Toll-free phone: 1-877-766-6776 Fax: (613) 592-7002 E-mail: 1-877-766-6777 Web site: www.somos.com	**Spearhead Management Canada Ltd.** 9 Antares Dr. Nepean ON K2E 7V5 Phone: (613) 226-4595 Fax: (613) 230-5739 E-mail: info@spearheadlimited.ca Web site: www.spearheadlimited.ca
Strategic Relationships Solutions Inc. Suite 901 275 Slater St. Ottawa ON K1P 5H9 Phone: (613) 233-4574 Fax: (613) 248-4514 E-mail: info@srscan.com Web site: www.srscan.com	**Systematix Solutions TI Inc.** Suite 920 333 Preston St. Ottawa ON K1S 5N4 Phone: (613) 567-8939 Fax: (613) 567-1916 E-mail: sciott@systematix.com Web site: www.systematix.com

T.E.S. Contract Services Inc. Suite 410 301 Moodie Dr. Nepean ON K2H 9C4 Phone: (613) 828-7887 Fax: (613) 828-2729 Toll-free fax: 1-800-818-5469 E-mail: ottawajobs@tes.net Web site: www.tes.net	**TDV Global Inc.** Suite 605 170 Laurier Ave. W. Ottawa ON K1P 5V5 Phone: (613) 231-8555 Fax: (613) 231-3970 E-mail: ottawa@tdvglobal.com Web site: www.tdvglobal.com
The 500 Staffing Inc. Suite 203 275 Slater St. Ottawa ON K1P 5H9 Phone: (613) 237-2888 Fax: (613) 237-2070 Toll-free fax: 1-866-307-9675 E-mail: prudhomme@the500.com Web site: www.the500.com	**The AIM Group Inc.** Suite 126 130 Albert St. Ottawa ON K1P 5G4 Phone: (613) 230-6991 Fax: (613) 230-7183 E-mail: info@theaimgroup.ca Web site: www.theaimgroup.ca/ottawa
The Corporate Research Group Ltd. Suite 325 301 Moodie Dr. Nepean ON K2H 9C4 Phone: (613) 596-2910 Fax: (613) 820-4718 Toll-free fax: 1-888-215-5147 E-mail: brianc@thecrg.com Web site: www.thecrg.com	**The Devon Group Ltd.** 887 Richmond Rd. Phone: (613) 567-2281 Fax: (613) 567-3693 E-mail: dwatss@devon.com Web site: www.devon.com
The Hicks Family Trust, The Ladouceur Family Trust, the Brulé Family Trust **(Emerion)** Suite 325 126 York St. Ottawa ON K1N 5T5 Phone: (613) 241-0222 Fax: (613) 241-2229 E-mail: cv@emerion.ca Web site: www.e-mergingsolutions.com	**Tiree Facility Solutions Inc.** Suite 301 1150 Morrison Dr. Ottawa ON K2H 8S9 Tel: (613) 222-2460 Fax: (613) 820-2867 E-mail: inquiry@tiree.ca Web site: www.tiree.ca

TPG Technology Consulting Ltd. Suite 100 887 Richmond Rd. Ottawa ON K2A 0G8 Phone: (613) 798-7647 Fax: (613) 798-7326 E-mail: (Online form) Web site: www.tpgtechnology.com	**Transpolar Technology Corporation** Suite 400 190 O'Connor St. Ottawa ON K2P 2R3 Phone: (613) 236-8108 E-mail: info@transpolar.com Web site: www.transpolar.com
TRM Technologies Inc. Suite 100 151 Slater St. Ottawa ON K1P 5H3 Phone: (613) 722-8843 Fax: (613) 722-8574 E-mail: info@trm.ca Web site: www.trm.ca	**Valcom Consulting Group Inc.** Suite 300 85 Albert St. Ottawa ON K1P 6A4 Phone: (613) 594-5200 Toll-free phone: 1-866-561-5580 Fax: (613) 233-0009 E-mail: info@valcom.ca Web site: www.valcom.ca
Wilcom Systems Ltd. Suite 110 887 Richmond Rd. Ottawa ON K2A 0G8 Phone: (613) 729-9211 Fax: (613) 729-4929 E-mail: angie.maher@wilcom.on.ca Web site: www.wilcomsystems.com